Stephanie Flood is a registered nurse who graduated from Calvin College in 1989. She devoted her entire nursing career to women and their families at one of the largest birthing centers in the Midwest. She was a bedside nurse and a charge nurse in Labor & Delivery.

She loves to spend time with her husband, adult children, and incredible grandchildren. She enjoys traveling and is a voracious reader. She meditates daily, is an avid cyclist, and is a seasoned yogi.

I dedicate this book to my husband, Randy. His unwavering love, encouragement and support were the driving force behind the creation and completion of this manuscript.

I also devote this book to my three adult children and their spouses, who have always believed in my capabilities and supported me in pursuing my goals.

And to my grandchildren, whose presence in my life has been the most precious and inspiring gift of all.

This book is also committed to my fellow Labor & Delivery nurses globally, and those who I had the privilege of working alongside locally, as they wholeheartedly devote themselves to pregnancy and birth. To the Obstetricians and Nurse Midwives with whom we share a close partnership. To the Scrub Techs who ensure our efficiency, and the Unit Secretaries who manage operations seamlessly.

Most importantly, this book is offered to all the patients and their families whom I had the honor of caring for throughout my career. Your trust and journeys were my daily inspiration.

Stephanie Flood, RN, BSN

WHEN THERE ARE TWO PATIENTS IN ONE BODY

A Nurse Shares Stories from the Delivery Room

AUSTIN MACAULEY PUBLISHERS
LONDON * CAMBRIDGE * NEW YORK * SHARJAH

Copyright © Stephanie Flood, RN, BSN 2025

All rights reserved. No part of this publication may be reproduced, distributed, or transmitted in any form or by any means, including photocopying, recording, or other electronic or mechanical methods, without the prior written permission of the publisher, except in the case of brief quotations embodied in critical reviews and certain other non-commercial uses permitted by copyright law. For permission requests, write to the publisher.

Any person who commits any unauthorized act in relation to this publication may be liable to criminal prosecution and civil claims for damages.

All of the events in this memoir are true to the best of author's memory. The views expressed in this memoir are solely those of the author.

Ordering Information
Quantity sales: Special discounts are available on quantity purchases by corporations, associations, and others. For details, contact the publisher at the address below.

Publisher's Cataloging-in-Publication data
Flood, RN, BSN, Stephanie
When There Are Two Patients in One Body

ISBN 9798889108214 (Paperback)
ISBN 9798889108221 (Hardback)
ISBN 9798889108245 (ePub e-book)
ISBN 9798889108238 (Audiobook)

Library of Congress Control Number: 2024927689

www.austinmacauley.com/us

First Published 2025
Austin Macauley Publishers LLC
40 Wall Street, 33rd Floor, Suite 3302
New York, NY 10005
USA

mail-usa@austinmacauley.com
+1 (646) 5125767

I would like to express my deepest gratitude to Maria Brummel-Schutte and Dr. Jeanette Thomas for their meticulous editing of each chapter in this book. Their assistance was instrumental in helping me to bring this book to a different level.

Thank you to my beta readers who contributed to making this book more readable and understandable. A big shoutout to: Randy, Maria, Melinda, Tina, Mary, Kirstin, Karaline, Janneke, Rick, Tim, Marie, Rachel, Vicki, Anna, Claire, Beth, Mark, Lisa, Nancy, Zach, Frank, Blair, and Vivian. Your feedback and support were invaluable.

I'd like to thank my niece, Gweneth Kelley, for her creativity in developing the original concept for the book cover and designing the tattoo sketches.

I also want to sincerely thank my writing coach, Chad R. Allen (*www.chadrallen.com*), for his guidance. With patience, he introduced me to the intricacies of publishing a book and taught me how to write my book proposal.

Table of Contents

Author's Note	**15**
Glossary	**19**
A List of Terms Pertaining to Childbirth	*19*
Introduction	**24**
Chapter 1: My Own First Experience With Birth	**26**
Chapter 2: Yellow Pajamas	**30**
Chapter 3: The Most Difficult Choice	**34**
Chapter 4: The Bradley Method	**39**
Chapter 5: We Both Knew	**45**
Chapter 6: Identical Twins	**49**
Chapter 7: An Icon. My Mentor.	**55**
Chapter 8: Abdominal Pregnancy	**57**
Chapter 9: "My Patients Aren't Dogs!"	**59**
Chapter 10: "You Think You're So Smart"	**63**
Chapter 11: Chain of Command	**66**
Chapter 12: Cradling the Cord	**70**

Chapter 13: French Kiss	74
Chapter 14: Not a Dry Eye	78
Chapter 15: HIV	82
Chapter 16: The Sound of Silence	85
Chapter 17: Postpartum Psychosis	88
Chapter 18: Hardened to Everything	91
Chapter 19: A Smell Like No Other	94
Chapter 20: Drenched With Sweat	98
Chapter 21: What Happens in Vegas	103
Chapter 22: Steadfast (In Her) Refusal	105
Chapter 23: We Just Played Together	109
Chapter 24: High Touch-Low Tech	113
Chapter 25: Praise Jesus	116
Chapter 26: While Pleading for Help	120
Chapter 27: Influenza A	123
Chapter 28: The Day Before Thanksgiving	127
Chapter 29: Never Judge a Book	133
Chapter 30: Abundant Faith	136
Chapter 31: They Have No Voice	141
Expected to Remain Silent	*141*
"If You Didn't Eat So Much Ice Cream"	*143*
Chapter 32: Babymoon	149
Chapter 33: Throuple	155

Chapter 34: Tattoos: A Collective Chapter	**158**
Epilogue	**168**
References	**173**

Crying does not indicate that you are weak. Since birth, it has been a sign that you are alive.

– Charlotte Bronte

Author's Note

In 2015, my husband and I visited Sedona, AZ where we stayed at a resort surrounded by the majestic Red Rocks and the most brilliant blue skies we had ever seen. Each day, as we hiked, music from a Native American Flutist cascaded down from his perch on a high cliff. The soothing ambient sound and early morning sun rays caused us to quickly lose sight of the accumulating miles. My mind started to revisit birth stories. As we traversed the trails, my excitement mounted as more and more narratives came into focus. The vivid details of each birth flowed out of my mouth as adrenaline churned with the cadence of each step. It was as if I had just given birth to a new idea, yet to be named. My husband suddenly stopped hiking, turned around and suggested, "why don't you write a book?" I still have the piece of paper with the resort letterhead where I jotted down my first list of stories.

While we were at the resort, we visited an intuitive life coach. After some time together, we began talking about my career, how I loved my work, but felt the need for something more, a new challenge, a way to impact others beyond the delivery room. I summoned the courage to mention the rather unconventional idea of my writing a book. I say unconventional because it felt so far removed from what I thought myself capable of at that time. Without hesitation, she encouraged me strongly, saying it was something I should seriously consider. She said, "clearly, you have a lot to share. Your face lights up when you begin talking. People would likely want to read it." My husband looked at me with an "I told you so" grin.

As we flew home and jumped back into our busy lives, the idea incubated. I continued to jot down the outlines of birth stories. When my husband bought a new computer for work, he gave me his old one and said, "Here, why don't you type out those stories?"

My mantra while writing this book has been: It has to be honest. This book is written for the whole human race, as everyone is connected to birth. It is not a memoir, but rather a collection of short vignettes intended to illustrate the human drama that acutely and remarkably manifests itself in the delivery room. The events are as they happened, with only names and some events being changed to protect the privacy of the patients. My personal reflections are in italics.

It is not my intent to scare the pregnant reader with these stories. The vast majority of the time, all goes well with labor, and most deliveries are like vanilla: smooth, beautiful and uneventful. Most of these stories are the exceptions, the rare cases. This book will offer you the truth of the varied human drama found in the delivery room.

In recounting these stories, I've worked to paint a clear and descriptive picture of the interactions I had with my patient and her family. To describe each birth with sensitivity and in as real and honest a way as possible. I share some of my inner thoughts and feelings that were sometimes raw and perhaps flawed. I strived to be professional, yet there is inherent vulnerability in my humanity.

According to Anthony de Mello, "You have to understand, my dears, that the shortest distance between truth and a human being is a story." Patients tell us their stories—whether it's with their mouths or with their actions, or a complicated combination of both. It goes without saying that each patient's story is entirely unique. In order to bring my best to each patient and family that I encountered, it was important that I listened to what they said, observed what might not be said, attempted to ask the right questions and then stay quiet, listen and pay attention. It was ***not*** my job to share my own story with them or insert my own values. I strived to approach each patient with a clean slate, with empathy and dignity, without prejudice, ensuring that my own filters did not mute or obscure their humanity or story. Though I didn't do it perfectly, setting that intention for my patient-nurse relationship was important to me and helped me provide the best care that I could.

Today, we live in a world where many people live out their lives in bubbles—closed networks of like-minded people who have shared experiences, outlooks, educational and socioeconomic levels, churches, news channels and communities. On Labor & Delivery, these bubbles collide. As a nurse caring for such a variety of different people, it was essential that I put my own thoughts and beliefs in the background so that I could care for *all* people, equitably and compassionately. Even, at times, when every part of me wanted to run out the door.

I worked in a large tertiary care center with one of the largest birthing centers in the Midwest, where an average of 8,000 deliveries occur each calendar year. The OB Triage unit has more patient volume than most emergency rooms and the neonatal ICU has a daily average census of 100 babies.

The standards of care have changed through the decades. Some of these cases happened more than 30 years ago and would have been handled very differently today, as the focus has become much more about patient safety. The policy changes also promote a culture of physical and emotional safety for the caregivers.

Glossary

A List of Terms Pertaining to Childbirth

1. **Full-Term Pregnancy** is 37–42 weeks. Any birth before 37 weeks is considered preterm. 34–37 weeks is late preterm, 28–33 weeks is moderately preterm and any pregnancy from 23 to 28 weeks is considered extremely premature. Usually, babies who are less than 22 weeks gestation cannot survive outside the womb and are considered non-viable.
2. **The Apgar Score,** introduced in 1952 by Dr. Virginia Apgar, measures how healthy a baby is at birth. It can be assigned by a nurse, a nurse practitioner or a physician. It is measured at one minute and five minutes after birth. It can range from 0–10, with 10 being best. Any score of 7 or greater is considered normal, four to six, fairly low and three or below are considered critically low. Any score less than 7 warrants immediate resuscitative efforts. (MedlinePlus, n.d.)
3. **Cesarean Section** is a surgical delivery of a baby through a cut (incision) made in the wall of the mother's abdomen and uterus.

4. **Normal Spontaneous Vaginal Delivery** (NSVD) is when a pregnant woman goes through labor and delivers her baby through the birth canal.
5. **Cervical Dilation and Stages of Labor:**
   a. The Latent Phase is the first stage of labor. Contractions are irregular and mild. This is considered the "waiting game" stage. This is when the cervix is dilated 1–4 centimeters (cm).
   b. The Active Phase of labor is the second stage, once the cervix is dilated 5 cm. Usually contractions are more regular, last longer and are stronger.
   c. Transition Phase is when the cervix dilates 7–10 cm. This is the most painful stage.
   d. For a vaginal delivery, a woman needs to be 10 centimeters dilated. Imagine the uterus as a balloon, with the cervix functioning like the balloon's neck and opening. As the woman progresses through the above mentioned phases of labor, the cervix stretches and widens, allowing the baby to pass through.
6. **Fetal Heart Rate (FHR) Categories:**
   a. Category I: This means that the baby's heart rate tracing is normal, formally called "reassuring".
   b. Normal FHR baseline is 110–160 beats per min (bpm).
   c. Category II is characterized by the absence of FHR variability and the presence of decelerations in the FHR. These are considered

indeterminate, non-reassuring and are a cause for concern. They require further evaluation, intervention and continued surveillance. They are a warning sign yet most pregnancies have at least one Category II tracing. They are associated with fetal metabolic acidosis.

    d. Category III fetal heart tracing is predictive of an abnormal fetal acid-base status, meaning that the fetus is not getting enough oxygen. Category III fetal heart tracings require immediate action and prompt delivery, usually via cesarean section.

7. **Fetal Auscultation**: Fetal auscultation involves periodically listening to the baby's heartbeat during pregnancy or labor. A Doppler is a handheld ultrasound device used for this purpose.

8. **Fetal Monitoring-External monitoring:** As the name implies, this monitoring happens on the outside of the mother's belly using an ultrasound transducer to trace the baby's heartbeat and a tocodynamometer (toco) to trace the frequency and duration of contractions. The toco cannot determine the strength of contractions.

9. **Fetal Monitoring-Internal monitoring:** This is fetal monitoring that can only be done when the mother's bag of water has been broken. It can involve a fetal scalp electrode (FSE) to trace the baby's heartbeat and/or an intrauterine pressure catheter (IUPC) to monitor the strength, length and frequency of uterine contractions.

10. **Umbilical Cord: What Blood Gases and pH Mean**
    a. Umbilical cord arterial pH is a measure of the fetal condition at birth.
    b. A low pH in newborns (acidosis) is caused by a lack of oxygen during labor or birth.
11. **OBSC-OB Special Care:** The inpatient unit in Women's Services dedicated to caring for patients who have high-risk/complicated pregnancies.
12. **PP-Postpartum**: The inpatient unit where patients and their babies stay for the duration of their hospitalization after childbirth.
13. **OB Triage**: This section of Labor & Delivery is often the patient's first contact with the hospital. This is where patients are evaluated. They are either admitted or sent home.
14. **L&D-Labor & Delivery:** a unit dedicated to caring for pregnant women during labor, delivery (both NSVD & C-section), and observation during pregnancies that are complicated.
15. **NICU-Neonatal Intensive Care Unit:** an intensive care unit dedicated to caring for newborn infants.
16. **Panda Warmer:** Panda Warmers are utilized in delivery rooms to immediately warm the baby as the nursing and neonatal teams assess the infant. The special warming properties allow the baby to stay unclothed and unwrapped while the team can easily assess and evaluate the baby and perform resuscitation if needed.

17. **Meconium** is the earliest stool of the unborn baby, composed of materials ingested during the time the infant spends in the uterus. Meconium is the dark, thick and sticky first poop of a newborn baby. Meconium can be passed after a baby is born or while still in the womb. Breathing in meconium (aspiration) can cause serious respiratory problems in the newborn (Cleveland Clinic, n.d.).

Introduction

It was a typical day in my life as a new parent. One Tuesday, my husband and I worked opposite shifts and my grandparents happily agreed to watch our young son for a few hours to cover the crossover. When I went to their house to collect my son after work, we had time to visit over a cup of coffee and catch up before I headed home.

As we sat down, my grandma (Eleanor) asked me, "How was your day today, honey?"

Now, mind you, I had been working as a Labor & Delivery nurse for (*maybe*) 6 months but I promptly responded, "Oh my God, Grandma, I have seen it all!"

Before I could even begin to tell her about my day, she interrupted me and said, "Stephanie, you will *NEVER* see it all." Her statement stopped me in my tracks. Looking back, I couldn't begin to tell you what the story was about, or if I even told it to them after that, but I have never forgotten my grandma's comment. Her words of wisdom have stuck with me throughout my nursing career. They became a cornerstone for the way I approached my job—keeping me open to all that unfolded each day.

When people learned what I did for my job, they would often respond, "You must have the best job ever!" What they often don't realize is that patients come to L&D filled with expectations, and also when they are at their most vulnerable and sometimes in crisis. The contrast of events that I have witnessed is why happiness can be so remarkable and grief so immense. The extent to which a birth event or experience can provide the heights of joy, loving connection and excitement—yes. But it also has the capacity to bring incredible levels of agony, despair and loss. As you can imagine, or may have experienced, all that we carry—our personal stories and the deep-seated dynamics of our relationships—has a way of showing up in the delivery room during the condensed, emotionally laden experience we call childbirth. As a Labor & Delivery nurse, I had the privilege of bearing witness to these life-changing events in people's lives.

I share these stories—the good and the bad of my decades of nursing and the thousands of babies I've helped deliver—as proof that my grandma Eleanor was right. I will never see it all. Welcome to Labor & Delivery.

Chapter 1
My Own First Experience With Birth

I graduated from high school in 1983 and, unbeknownst to me at the time, I was 18 weeks pregnant. I had missed several periods but ignored that fact. I told myself that it was simply because I was on the track team and had been running so much. Who wants to grapple with the stark reality of an unplanned pregnancy in the final lap of your senior year of high school? Not me.

My first prenatal visit happened around 20 weeks, when the power of denial was overtaken by the protruding reality of jeans that wouldn't zip, five missed periods, and a bra cup size that had more than doubled.

I was raised in a small town and attended a very conservative church. Premarital sex and certainly, pregnancy before marriage, were deeply frowned upon. The only birth control discussed was abstinence and abortion was strictly forbidden. Therefore, sex education *wasn't* needed and I naively thought I could only get pregnant when I was on my period. Instead of offering support when my pastor found out I was pregnant, he told me to be sure that I didn't wear white on my wedding day, should I ever *actually* marry. According to him, I was damaged goods. I was not involved with the baby's father.

Because I was pregnant, I did not go to college the fall after my high-school graduation, as I had always planned. Instead, I lived with my mother (a pharmacist who battled addictions), my twin brother and my younger sister. My parents divorced when I was in middle school. My father, also a pharmacist, had moved to Texas to pursue his dream of becoming a physician's assistant. Other than significant depression, weight gain and unemployment, my pregnancy was uneventful.

I went into labor six days before my due date. I spent the first six hours of early labor at home with my 20-year-old sister who was married with two boys of her own. She also struggled with her own early, addictive behaviors. She was going to be my labor coach.

I didn't know if I was having a boy or a girl but I had already decided that I was going to give my baby up for adoption. I did not have a family safety net. My gut, my intuition that has served me well, told me that my home was no place to raise a child. I was essentially on my own. My mom was struggling with her own addiction, and my dad had moved to Texas. I clung to the faith that permitted me to love my baby in the most counterintuitive way: rather than hold onto her, I had to let her go.

When I got to the hospital at midnight, I was in active labor. My labor progressed as is typical for a first baby. Ten hours after arriving at a small rural hospital, I was completely dilated (10 cm) and my contractions were regular and very painful. The only pain control that I was offered was one intramuscular shot of a narcotic called Demerol and Vistaril (an anti-nausea medication). It helped me relax but it certainly didn't take the pain away. They never started an IV. The barely legible handwritten hospital records say that I was complete and pushy but the baby's head was high in my pelvis. At 10:30 that morning, the on-call doctor, a family medicine physician, finally broke my water. The amniotic fluid was clear and five minutes later I was transferred to a delivery room.

I have no recollection of pushing but I remember that the room was big, sterile and very cold. Without explanation or justification—and without asking for my consent—an episiotomy was performed and low outlet forceps (imagine large metal salad tongs) were used to pull my baby out, while using only lidocaine for local anesthetic. It was traumatic and barbaric: I never knew that such physical agony was possible. I vividly remember thinking that my innards were being pulled out. It felt as though I was being punished for having a baby when I was 18 and out of wedlock.

My daughter came into this world, cone-headed, swollen and suffering from a fractured right clavicle. I held and cared for her in the hospital as much as I could because I knew that the three days I was hospitalized would be the only time I got to spend with her. I proceeded with a closed adoption and left the hospital with very empty arms.

My heart ached. Family and friends came to the hospital to visit and offer support, but it was my nurse, Karen, who made the whole ordeal tolerable. She sat with me, held my hand and listened as I cried and spoke of my fears, my hopes for my daughter's future, and my uncertainty about my own fate. How could I possibly give my baby up for adoption? How could I raise her? I was a single, 18-year-old high-school graduate from a home broken by divorce and addiction. Karen believed in me. She told me that whatever choice I made, I would make the best of it. She encouraged me to go to college as planned and to perhaps even become a nurse. She touched me deeply.

The birth of our children is one of the most vulnerable times of our lives. Now that I too am a nurse, I often think of Karen and my first baby as I sit with my own patients, listening to their stories of hope, their worst fears, their goals and best laid plans. Karen had a significant impact on my life, and what I learned from her I have tried to carry forward to my patients. I have been in Women's Services since 1989 and have attended thousands of births. People regularly tell me, "You have such a great job." The reality is that, most of the time, they are right.

The human endeavor of attraction, partnering, intimacy, pregnancy, and birthing *is* powerfully dramatic, but often messy and certainly not always idyllic.

Chapter 2
Yellow Pajamas

I had just finished a 12-hour shift that still, 30 years later, goes down as one of the worst I had ever worked. It was one of those days. It was flu season and several nurses had called in sick. Which, in retrospect, meant that we had more patients than we could safely handle and far fewer than the normal number of nurses to take care of them. At 7:45 p.m., I had finally finished giving report to the nurse who was taking over my patient. I was eager to get home to cuddle my own young children before they went to sleep.

As I walked past the main desk on my way to the locker room, I overheard the charge nurse discussing a patient who had been up on OB Special Care (OBSC). This patient was 40 years old and 40 weeks pregnant with her second baby. She had been admitted in preparation for her induction of labor.

The nurse on OBSC had run her evening fetal monitor strip at 6:30 p.m. and was concerned that "the baby didn't look good". She took the monitor off and the decision was made to transfer the patient to Labor & Delivery, despite how busy we were at the time. Given that we were low on staff and in the midst of shift change, there was no nurse available yet to care for this patient. The charge nurse reluctantly asked me, "Hey Steph, can you please just go put the new patient on the monitor? I'll watch her fetal heart tones from here until someone can take over her care."

I never wanted to say "No" more than I did at that moment. The mere thought of smiling and being nice to one more patient seemed impossible. I hadn't eaten anything for hours and had hardly any water to drink all day. *My breath might hurt this patient*, I thought. My brain and my body were spent. But, I knew it was the right thing to do, so I went back down the hall to put her on the monitor. I didn't even know this woman's name. I could barely remember my own.

To say that I was stunned by my first impression would be an understatement. When I walked into her room, she was sitting cross-legged on the bed that hadn't even had the top sheet pulled back for her. The bed was still elevated from when it was cleaned last. I'm not sure how she got her heavily pregnant body up that high. She was strikingly beautiful. Her hair was perfectly colored and coiffed, her lips, fingernails and toenails were painted bright candy-apple red. Her skin was porcelain, flawless. Her two-piece pajama set was a lovely, brilliant yellow with large, white pearl buttons. The diamonds in her ears were easily two carats each. She looked like she belonged on the cover of a Vogue magazine.

She must have been equally as stunned by my exhausted, disheveled appearance.

I just wanted to put her baby on the monitor so I could go home. I introduced myself and found out her name was Susan. Her husband Tom was home with their two-year-old son. He would be coming later once the induction of labor was started.

I put the monitor on and, immediately, my adrenaline started to rush. This baby had Category III fetal heart tones, which at the time were referred to as "non-reassuring fetal heart tones". Her baby was in big trouble. The baseline fetal heart rate was 150 with absent (no) variability. Her tracing looked like I had drawn a straight line with a pencil. Susan didn't know she was having contractions, but her baby sure did. The repetitive late decelerations were deep and wide after each contraction. This is a sign of severe fetal distress. Steps needed to be taken immediately to deliver this baby. So much for going home. And so much for Susan's yellow pajamas.

I quickly put the call bell on and asked for the OB resident to come to the room STAT. Also, someone needed to page her obstetrician to come to the hospital immediately as I knew that he was at home. I also asked for an IV and other necessary supplies for a C-section. I told Susan that I was very concerned that her baby was in trouble. The resident told her that she would need to be delivered by emergency cesarean section. Her cervix had been checked by the OB resident earlier that day and she was only dilated to 1 cm. The hope for a vaginal delivery, like her first son, was not plausible and I explained to her that this baby wasn't tolerating the contractions she didn't even feel, let alone the active labor that would be needed to dilate her cervix to 10 cm. She looked me square in the eye and said, "I don't want a C-section."

Had I not already worked now going on 13 terrible hours, my response may have been kinder and softer. I *thought* to myself, *I don't want to do a C-section right now either. I just worked 13 hours from hell and I want to go home. Your baby is dying on the monitor as we speak and we really don't have a choice. Just do what I say and for God's sake, don't argue with me!*

Instead, as I was starting her IV and drawing her blood, I told her very directly, "If we don't do a C-section right now, your baby will die. Your baby's heartbeat is telling us that he is very distressed." She reluctantly agreed and called her husband. Her doctor arrived and we quickly proceeded to the operating room where we delivered a very compromised baby boy, whose Apgar scores were very low. His arterial cord pH was 6.7 and he went to the neonatal intensive care unit (NICU) on a ventilator just as her husband, Tom, arrived.

The demands of my job, the juxtaposition between my desire to go home and the necessity to remain at work, forced me to face this unexpected crisis. Even though it wouldn't typically have been my responsibility since I had already completed my 12-hour shift, I felt obligated to stay and take care of this patient. I eventually left for home at 11:00 p.m.

In reflection, I realize that there is a vivid contrast between my perspective and Susan's during this unanticipated obstetrical crisis. My own dismay and temporary inconvenience were minor compared to the upheaval Susan must have felt. I recognize that different people may experience the same situation in vastly different ways.

Chapter 3
The Most Difficult Choice

It was a bright sunny day in mid-July. I had slept well and woke up refreshed. I decided on my drive to work to make that day a great one! I would grab a quick cup of coffee and do a fifteen minute walk around the hospital, a routine that I cherished. It was a very helpful tool for clearing my mind. A form of meditation, long before I knew what that really meant.

There was a large dry erase whiteboard in the center of the nurses station. Down the left-hand side of the board was a list of all of the patient room numbers. Across the top of the board were multiple columns. These included the patient's initials, her doctor's name, how far she was dilated, what number baby she was having, and finally, an open space for any other pertinent patient information. Every day, before our shift began, the nurses were allowed to sign up for the patient of her choice from that board. It was first come, first served.

When I walked up to the board, I saw that someone had already signed me up for a patient. This was unusual, so I asked the charge nurse about it. She explained that the patient's doctor, whom I had worked closely with many times before, had chosen me specifically to take care of this patient. The charge nurse explained, "Tracy is scheduled to be induced at 7:30 a.m. and is not here yet. Dr. Baker would like to talk to you before you admit her patient. I'll page her for you now."

I changed into my scrubs, grabbed some coffee and headed to the doctor's lounge to connect with Dr. Baker, accepting that my walk would have to wait.

Dr. Baker told me that Tracy was 35 years old, married to Aaron. She was 34 weeks pregnant with their third baby and planning to be induced that day, six weeks before her Labor Day due date.

Tracy had discovered a lump in her breast when she was barely 9 weeks pregnant. A mammogram, breast ultrasound and subsequent biopsy of the large tumor revealed an aggressive type of breast cancer that had already spread to her lymph nodes. Because she was pregnant, she was quickly referred to an oncologist. This breast care specialist told her and Aaron that they would have to make a wretched choice. To increase Tracy's chance of survival, she would need to have a double mastectomy and begin chemotherapy and radiation as soon as possible, but in order to do so and improve Tracy's prognosis and chance of survival, she would have to terminate her pregnancy. This type of cancer was made worse by the hormones of pregnancy and the chemo/radiation treatments would gravely harm the unborn fetus.

They were stunned, speechless. Barely able to grasp what they were being told. They left the office and promised to return within one week with their decision. They needed time alone, then time with their families and ultimately their pastor.

Tracy and Aaron had two daughters at home, ages three and five. They belonged to a small church in their neighborhood and their faith was of utmost importance to them. They prayed, cried, prayed some more. Hoping to find peace with a decision to this unspeakable dilemma: Terminate their pregnancy so that Tracy could begin treatment and have the best chance to survive and raise their two daughters. If they chose *this* option, their baby would be gone and she was told she shouldn't ever be pregnant again. OR she could stay pregnant, have the double mastectomy, deliver the baby early and then start chemo/radiation after the delivery. This course, and delay in treatment, would increase the likelihood of metastasis (further spread of the cancer to other parts of her body) and decrease the probability of her survival. This could potentially leave Aaron to single-parent three motherless children.

After prayer and discernment and many sleepless nights of crying and clinging to each other, they decided that terminating the pregnancy was not an option for them. Tracy underwent a double mastectomy and the pregnancy was relatively normal until she began experiencing terrible headaches and some shortness of breath. Testing showed that the cancer had spread to her brain and her lungs.

Leaving the doctor's lounge, my mind was racing. How could I possibly take care of them, help bring a beautiful new life into this world, all while embracing their pain and the reality that most assuredly, Tracy would not be present at this new baby's first birthday party? Honestly, I wasn't sure I could handle the task of being fully open and fully vulnerable, able to help carry their collective grief and joy.

Tracy and Aaron arrived promptly at 7:30 a.m. When I went in to meet them and admit Tracy, Dr. Baker was already in the room, sitting on Tracy's bed, holding her hand. They were all crying. I stood beside Dr. Baker and put my hand on her shoulder. She introduced me to Tracy and Aaron. I nodded and then I started to cry. After a few long moments, Tracy looked at me and said, "It's nice to meet you, Stephanie. Now that we've all cried, we can move on and start my induction. I have a daughter to meet. Her name will be Angela as she will always be our angel."

Tracy's labor progressed quickly despite the fact that she was six weeks from her due date. Angela was truly angelic. Beautiful, wide-eyed and feisty. She went to NICU because of her prematurity but we were all hopeful that her stay there would be short so that Tracy could mother her as much, and as quickly, as possible.

Tracy died peacefully three months later, at home, surrounded by Aaron, their parents and her three angels.

I likely would not have taken this patient so early in my career, because of fear that I would not have been able to hold myself together. I am thankful that Dr. Baker believed in me, saw attributes in me that at the time, I couldn't see in myself, and requested my presence. I accepted this assignment. I chose to let my faith speak louder than my fear and I became a better nurse because of it. I realized that in life, we can prepare ourselves to do difficult things or we can choose to avoid that which makes us uncomfortable. There are also times we are thrust into situations by circumstance or invitation, being afforded the opportunity to respond with our best selves, rather than letting fear and self-doubt rule.

Chapter 4
The Bradley Method

The Bradley Method is a philosophy that birth is a natural process where the emphasis is on partner-coached childbirth. Mothers are encouraged to trust their own bodies, to keep a strong focus on eating a healthy diet and to exercise regularly throughout their pregnancy. Couples are taught that mothers should manage labor by deep breathing and relying heavily on the support of her birth partner. Natural childbirth is, according to the Bradley Method, simply giving birth naturally—using deep relaxation and controlled breathing techniques, instead of medication, to manage labor pain.

Kayla and Michael were in their early 30s, educated, thoughtful and fully indoctrinated in the Bradley Method. They attended classes and seminars, did extensive research and wrote a birth plan detailing exactly how they expected the delivery of their first baby to unfold. Kayla was fit, healthy and had no risk factors so they couldn't fathom any reason why their hospital team wouldn't be fully supportive of their requests.

Their written birth plan went like this:

1. Allow Kayla to eat and drink whatever sounds good to her, at any time (they brought their own food/drinks).
2. Occasional fetal heart rate checks by doppler only would be allowed. (Regular, continuous bedside fetal monitoring was unnecessary and out of the question.)
3. Allow Kayla to move freely around the room, with or without clothing, depending on how uncomfortable (or hot) labor makes her.
4. Allow Kayla to shower or take a whirlpool bath as needed for relaxation or pain control.
5. No vaginal exams from her physician, and certainly not from her nurse. She will let you know when it's time to push, and will then consider an exam.
6. No IV and DO NOT OFFER any pain medications or labor epidural.

There was an equally extensive birth plan for after the baby was born (e.g., exclusive breastfeeding, no bottles or formula, no medications or immunizations of any kind, skin to skin, rooming in, all newborn exams done at the parents' bedside, etc.). Birth plans are doable when everything goes smoothly, but ironically, the longer and more extensive the birth plan, in my experience, unfortunately, the more problems a patient seemed likely to encounter.

Kayla's labor was neither perfect nor smooth. By the time she came to the hospital, she was already exhausted from 36 hours of early, consistent labor at home. She thought her water may have broken the day before, but would not allow staff to verify this important detail. Nor would she allow a vaginal exam to see how far she was dilated. To her, it didn't matter because she was in labor. She and Michael did consent to a 20-minute fetal monitor strip while the admission questions were being asked and the birth plan reviewed, but the monitor was to remain off for the duration of her labor after that.

Their baby had a different take on things. During the 20-minute fetal monitor strip, the baby's heart rate showed decreased variability and no accelerations. Thankfully, there were no decelerations, so no immediate intervention was needed, but her physician wanted to keep the monitor on, just to be safe. A portable monitor was offered so Kayla could remain mobile, but she and Michael refused all of it. It didn't fit into their birth plan.

Although several important labor questions remained unanswered, Kayla was taken off the monitor and transferred to a labor room. She was ten days past her due date and having regular contractions that she and Michael were working hard to breathe through. They were fiercely determined to proceed as planned.

I was the first nurse Michael didn't fire. By the time I entered the scene, the wildfire of Michael's determined support of Kayla—interested only in practicing Bradley Method techniques—had burned through several of my co-workers. When any nurse didn't honor Kayla's birth plan to a T, she was asked to leave the room and not return. The longer Kayla was in labor, the quieter she got and the louder and more objectionable Michael became.

Concerns about Kayla's labor and the health of their unborn baby grew. Prior nurses had suggested interventions such as continuous fetal monitoring, IV fluids to prevent dehydration and changes in Kayla's position in bed. Michael became adamant that staff leave them alone and let them labor as planned. He was furious when Kayla's doctor began to suggest the need for a C-section, even after sharing the multiple reasons why he believed it to be the safest option for them and their baby.

Several more times, Michael refused the C-section, all while Kayla was becoming so exhausted that she could hardly move her body or breathe through the contractions. She no longer had the energy to move around the room and she reluctantly agreed to continuous fetal monitoring. Alarmingly, she was leaking foul-smelling amniotic fluid and had still not had a vaginal exam. We had no idea how far she was dilated or what position her baby was in.

After patiently caring for them for several hours, adhering to their birth plan as closely as possible, I sat with them and did my best to explain that they had done everything they could to birth this baby naturally. I assured them that they had done everything right. It took what felt like an hour before they realized that their birth might not go as planned.

During all of this, the fetal monitor began to show an ominous strip. The baby needed to be delivered. Kayla's physician pleaded with her to consent to a C-section, which she finally did—possibly more out of sheer exhaustion than anything else. Kayla could barely muster the energy to speak, but she whispered her consent. Michael was intransigent and refused the C-section yet again. It wasn't until the baby's heart rate dropped into the 50s, and stayed there, that he finally relented. Ten minutes later, a very compromised baby girl was born and transferred immediately to NICU.

Michael's only response, "See…we should have just delivered at home!"

When it was all over, I sat with my head in my hands, remembering the countless times I had witnessed all-natural childbirths that had gone exactly as planned. (My own included among the many. I chose an all-natural birth with my son, my second baby. During my labor, we listened to Enya's Watermark, on repeat, on the cassette tape. My husband was a steady, stabilizing force. He rubbed my back, where most of my labor pain was. He supported me through one contraction at a time, all while he was silently thankful that he wasn't going through this whole birthing process. Fortunately, it worked for me.)

I came to learn throughout my career that this determination is one of the most necessary, yet often not sufficient, predictors of success in this venture of natural childbirth. You have to want it more than anything, including the seductive, enticing offers of pain control. As a former patient myself, I understand it (the Bradley Method). As a L&D nurse, I struggled with this rigidity at times. Especially when the baby has a different plan, as shown by fetal distress or unfavorable presentation.

I was aware of feeling a combination of: **Sadness**: *(sometimes labor just doesn't go as planned, no matter how prepared we are)* **Frustration**: *(Michael, why are you being so obstinate? Why won't you listen to and trust your care providers?)* **Anger**: *(Kayla and the baby could have been spared so much suffering had she delivered sooner)*

Gratitude: *(Michael could have fired me as their nurse, as he had several others, but he didn't. This at least gave me the chance to make a difference for them and their unborn daughter).*

I am also aware that as humans, we are the only species who enter the birth process with a plan. In the hospital, we are sometimes able to alter a catastrophic labor course with medical intervention. Yet, as humans, we sometimes cling to our idyllic narratives even when our babies and bodies scream out for us to hit the delete button and begin rewriting.

Chapter 5
We Both Knew

Nancy was in active labor when I took over her care at 3:00 p.m. on a hot summer afternoon in July. She was dilated to 7 cm and she was 39+ weeks pregnant. Her water broke early that morning at home while she was getting ready for work as an RN in the neonatal intensive care unit (NICU). Her husband Nate was tall, sharply dressed, soft-spoken and very supportive at her bedside.

Nancy was comfortable with her epidural and our connection was instantaneous. She spoke fondly of Tessa, her two-year-old daughter, who was home with Nate's parents, anxiously awaiting the arrival of her "bruvver" or "baby sista". Nancy and Nate did not know the gender of their baby and had no preference for boy or girl. They just wanted a healthy baby.

Their daughter, Tessa, was an easy vaginal delivery. Nancy's current pregnancy had been "a piece of cake" and this delivery turned out to follow the exact path as her first, only easier and faster. At 6:15 p.m., Nancy woke up from a catnap and felt a sudden urge to push. She was completely dilated so I called her physician to come for the delivery.

While we waited for the doctor to arrive, we chatted and waged final gender bets as I made some last-minute room preparations.

At 6:38 p.m., just 2 pushes later, Nancy delivered a bald, crying baby girl. They were overjoyed to welcome their daughter Olivia into their family.

Nate was crying happy tears while the physician was delivering the placenta and checking if any repairs needed to be done. Nancy and I were both silent, alternating between looking at Olivia and looking at each other. Neither of us spoke the words we both wanted to say and Nancy started to cry. I asked if I could take the baby to the warmer to do an assessment and she willingly handed her daughter over to me.

My own tears burned behind my eyelids. My heart was beating fast and my sweat took on a nervous odor. This baby had good color but poor muscle tone. She had a large tongue that she kept sticking out of her mouth. She had wide hands with short fingers and a deep simian crease across the palm of each hand. Her big and second toes had a deep groove between them and her ink footprints would ultimately look like a capital V. Her sweet eyes were alert but almond-shaped and her small ears were low set.

I knew, as did Nancy, that Olivia most likely had Trisomy 21 or Down's Syndrome. This had not been diagnosed during her pregnancy and Nate was not yet aware.

The night nurse came into the room to relieve me and finish Nancy's recovery. I introduced her to Nancy, Nate and baby Olivia and gave her a bedside report, leaving out my suspicion of Down's Syndrome. I said goodbye and congratulations to the new family and left the room. I went out to the desk with the night nurse where I shared my concerns about the baby. She had noticed and was in agreement. I paged the pediatrician to give her the news and to see if she wanted any special testing done that night or if she would just round on the baby in the morning. She chose the latter and the night nurse would tell Nancy.

I cried most of the way home that night, not because Olivia likely had Down's Syndrome. She was born to parents who would, without a doubt, love and take the very best care of her. I cried because I hadn't summoned the courage to talk about my observations while in the room with them. I cried because Nate didn't know the news that was coming the next day.

Needless to say, I didn't get much sleep that night.

The next day, I went to visit Nancy, Nate and Olivia up on the Postpartum floor. When I walked in the room, all four grandparents and their daughter Tessa were present. As soon as I made eye contact with Nancy, we both started to cry. I sat on her bed and we hugged and cried together. I apologized for avoiding the truth with them the night before. I wished I had a do-over and I told them so.

Before Nancy could speak, her mother looked at me and said, "Stephanie, I've heard wonderful things about you. It's nice to meet you. And don't you worry about Miss Olivia. She's going to be fine. We're all going to be fine."

I believe she spoke the truth.

Throughout my career, I frequently took care of high-risk, complicated cases, but I had to learn how to have tough conversations with patients and their families. I knew what to do with the messiness of blood and bodily fluids, as that is what it takes for babies to make their appearance, but I didn't have the same comfort with delivering hard truths. That confidence grew over the years—as I matured, gained more experience and saw more of life. What I discovered early in my career is that childbearing also gives birth to powerful emotions, reveals character, and showcases relationship dynamics. It was my job to recognize and muster the courage to take care of all of them.

Chapter 6
Identical Twins

Sarah was a petite, 19-year-old woman. Her husband Anthony was in his early 20s. From the very beginning of her pregnancy, Sarah had planned on an "all-natural" birth, with only intermittent fetal monitoring and no other interventions. She was healthy and without any known health risks. At her 20-week ultrasound, Sarah and Anthony were elated to discover that they were expecting not one, but two daughters.

As was typical, Sarah saw a variety of resident obstetricians for her prenatal visits at the hospital OB clinic. Once it was known that she was having twins, each of the residents consistently advised against her "all-natural" plan, given that twin pregnancies are inherently high-risk. But, nevertheless, she held fast to her decision.

At her 34-week ultrasound, she learned that Baby A (the baby who would deliver first) had moved into the breech position, while Baby B remained cephalic—head down. This is one of the riskiest configurations for twins to be in, as there are increased chances of problems during delivery. She was still doing great with her pregnancy and remained adamant that she wanted an "all-natural" birth. Her care providers counseled her about the risks of a vaginal breech delivery, especially because it was her first birth *and* because two babies were involved. Ultimately, the physicians would not consent to her wishes because the inherent risks were too great, even in the best of circumstances.

As a result, Sarah and Anthony decided to discontinue their prenatal care with the OB clinic. They searched all over the area for an obstetrician or Certified Nurse Midwife who would honor their requests for a non-interventional hospital twin birth. Their search was unsuccessful and they eventually decided on a planned home birth with a lay midwife.

The babies were born on a snowy Saturday in February when Sarah was 37 weeks pregnant. Amazingly, Baby A delivered at home without incident, in the frank breech position. Baby B was still cephalic (head down). Several minutes later, Baby A was breastfeeding when Sarah's water broke spontaneously for Baby B. Unfortunately, before the baby's head could settle into the cervix, the umbilical cord fell into the vagina in front of the baby's head (otherwise known as a cord prolapse), therefore cutting off oxygen to the baby.

The lay midwife instructed Sarah to push to get the baby out. She pushed, with the umbilical cord hanging from her vagina, for approximately 15 minutes before the midwife decided that it was time for them to all go to the hospital. They rode with the midwife in her car. They did not call an ambulance. (If this cord prolapse had happened during a hospital twin delivery, she would have been rushed into the operating room for an emergency cesarean delivery of Baby B.)

I was the charge nurse on our unit the day their home birth failed. I received a phone call from the emergency room (ER) charge nurse that a patient had just arrived. He said, "She has one baby in her arms and one still on the way with an umbilical cord hanging out." We didn't know any other details but immediately strung an IV and opened our operating room.

Around the corner came Sarah, screaming from pain, hysterical with fear. Anthony was carrying Baby A in his arms. Baby B was stuck in Sarah's birth canal with the umbilical cord dangling between her legs. Their midwife was with them, her long hair in two braids down her back, dressed in denim overalls, a flannel shirt and Birkenstock sandals—she was covered in Sarah's blood.

We moved Sarah onto a labor bed and attempted to find fetal heart tones. We were unsuccessful, unsure if this was due to fetal distress (or death) or due to Sarah's movement and screaming. The midwife quickly gave us a rundown of events as we started an IV and got verbal consent from Sarah to do an emergency cesarean section. We told the midwife and Anthony that we were taking Sarah to the operating room immediately to deliver Baby B.

The midwife assumed that she and Anthony would be joining us in the operating room. When I told her that Sarah would be put under general anesthesia and that, per hospital policy, no one would be allowed to accompany her, she looked at me, hands on her hips, and said, "Sarah is my patient and I'm going with her!"

I informed her that Sarah was no longer her patient and that under no circumstances could she go with us. Only Anthony would have been able to come if it weren't for the general anesthesia. I expressed to her the urgency of the situation and that I was very concerned about the well-being of the baby. She put her hands on her hips, looked me squarely in the eye and said angrily, "I've *NEVER* lost a baby yet."

Before leaving for the operating room, I quietly responded, "Hell NO you haven't, because you bring them to us and we lose them."

The OB and NICU teams were ready when we rolled into the operating room. We moved Sarah onto the operating room table and before doing anything else, the attending physician wanted to check Sarah and have her do one trial push before proceeding with a cesarean section. She followed his direction and quickly proceeded to deliver her second daughter vaginally, with very little assistance and no anesthesia. Sarah and Anthony had beautiful identical twin daughters, both born with fair skin and curly black hair.

Baby B had Apgar scores of 0–0–1. There is a Labor & Delivery motto: "6.9 is just in time" and "6.8 is too late". This baby's umbilical cord pH was just 6.7. After a lengthy resuscitation, she was transferred to the NICU where she died the next day. Our whole team was distraught. This loss was unnecessary and avoidable.

We took Sarah back to her room. When Sarah and Anthony initially arrived at the hospital, they refused to allow us to admit Baby A, which was necessary to provide care and keep her with Sarah. They assumed they would all four go home immediately after the birth of Baby B. However, once the ominous outlook of Baby B started to sink in, they agreed to allow us to admit Baby A. I don't think they had *any* idea yet that Baby B would die less than 24 hours after her birth from hypoxic ischemic encephalopathy (HIE), brain damage caused by lack of oxygen, which in this case was caused by the prolonged prolapse and compression of the umbilical cord.

About an hour after Baby A was admitted, she was under the Panda Warmer and I was performing a standard newborn assessment. She was crying, as newborns do, while I gave her a bath and washed her hair. Sarah looked at me and angrily said, "Stop it, you're making her cry!"

I asked her if she wanted me to stop the bath and just dress the baby, and she said, "Yes!"

I did as she asked and as I handed that beautiful baby girl back to her, all I could think of was the fact that her second daughter would never cry.

I do not share this story to condemn home birthing. There is inherent tension between the home birth, all-natural, hands-off birthing philosophy and in-hospital birthing where interventions are common and sometimes happen when perhaps they shouldn't. I would like to tip my hat to the countless women and midwives who have had wonderful, smooth deliveries in the comforts of home. I know they are common, and most of the time, they go very well, without complications.

It's like housework—you only notice it when it's not done. Home births are only in the limelight when they fail to go as planned. I believe it is also important to acknowledge that certain risk factors (in this case, a twin pregnancy) and pregnancy complications make it inherently unsafe to deliver outside of the hospital.

It is also prudent to acknowledge that, over the past 25 years, there has been a significant shift in the vaginal breech delivery recommendations. Therefore, there are fewer and fewer providers with this skill set, much less a first twin.

Chapter 7
An Icon. My Mentor.

My mentor was an icon in our circle of obstetricians. He was a tall, skinny man who was very connected to the women he took care of. He knew every patient's name without looking at the chart, her mother, her sister and her granny's name. He knew the daughter, the niece and the cousin. He had delivered them as babies and then, their babies. He practiced for 34 years and by the time he retired, he told me he had delivered 11,000+ babies.

He had a calm but commanding presence, making his soft words easily heard, even in a room full of visitors. He was rarely argued with because, most of the time, he was right. He routinely predicted the time his patient would deliver (he was usually correct within minutes). He had a very low C-section rate—never doing a C-section for his own convenience. If he said his patient needed a cesarean, we knew it wasn't about a tee time, an evening commitment or a holiday party, but rather, that it was truly needed.

Dr. Mather expected his patients to call him first with any issues or complaints before going to the hospital. He wanted to know what was happening with them and to be in charge of the decision about whether or not they should be seen at the hospital in OB, in the emergency room, wait to be seen at his office during office hours or to stop being ridiculous and take a nap. His patients knew not to show up in OB Triage without calling him first, unless they were about to give birth. When they didn't follow this expectation, they, along with their mothers and sisters, risked being reprimanded by him. Although he was paternalistic, his patients sought his care and respected his advice and counsel.

These are three stories about my work with this incredible physician. I admire him greatly but that doesn't mean he was *always* easy to work with.

Chapter 8
Abdominal Pregnancy

Sherica was 34 weeks pregnant with her third baby when she showed up unannounced in OB Triage. Her abdominal pain started at 5:00 a.m. when she got up to empty her bladder. It was now 6:00 a.m. and she was writhing in pain. She was also terribly nauseated, which was unusual for her.

When the triage nurse put the external fetal monitor on, she noticed the peculiar shape of Sherica's abdomen. It was shaped like a peanut laying sideways across her belly. Very odd. The baby's heart tones were found in the left upper quadrant of Sherica's abdomen, when they would normally be found beneath her belly button. Again, very odd. The abdomen was taut and very tender to the touch. The nurse could see the outline of the baby's body. None of this was normal.

The nurse called Dr. Mather right away because she knew that if he hadn't called to say that Sherica was coming in, he didn't know she was there.

When her doctor walked quietly into Sherica's room, he was mad that she hadn't called him directly. He crossed his arms and said, "What you acting like this for? This isn't your first baby!" The nurse got out a glove and some lubricant so that he could do a vaginal exam to see how far she was dilated. After putting his fingers in her vagina to do the exam, he quickly pulled them out and calmly but clearly stated, "We need to do a C-section right now." It was completely out of the ordinary for him to call a stat C-section from OB Triage, especially on an actively laboring woman who had already had two prior vaginal deliveries.

In the operating room, Sherica was put under general anesthesia and the neonatal team was ready to assume care for her premature baby. Dr. Mather was known for his uncanny ability, in an emergency, to get to a baby with one swipe of his scalpel. With Sherica, he made the skin incision, worked his way quickly through the second fascial layer and then stopped in his tracks. The baby was moving around inside the placental sac, inside the peritoneum, outside of the uterus.

He told us later that when he had examined Sherica earlier, he could feel how displaced her cervix was. His gut told him that something was very wrong, and he was very right. This was an abdominal pregnancy—an extremely rare occurrence. In the United States, 1–2% of pregnancies are ectopic pregnancies, caused when a fertilized egg implants somewhere other than the uterus, commonly in the fallopian tube. Of those 1–2%, about 1.4% are abdominal ectopic pregnancies.

Both Sherica and her baby were lucky; they both survived and thrived. A true miracle, one in millions.

Chapter 9
"My Patients Aren't Dogs!"

I was still a fairly new Labor & Delivery nurse when Serena came into OB Triage. She was actively laboring with her second baby, a few days after her due date. She was dilated to 6–7 cm upon arrival to the hospital and she wasn't tolerating labor very well. The triage nurse let Dr. Mather know that Serena had arrived and that she wanted an epidural. He ordered that she be transferred to a labor room and said, "She doesn't need an epidural. Just have the resident break her water and I'll be there at 3:00 to deliver her." We all rolled our eyes, knowing that likely, he'd be spot-on with her delivery time and that Serena would be very upset about not being able to get her epidural.

Around 1:30 p.m., the resident came to the room to check on Serena and to break her water. She was dilated 7–8 cm and was, as we predicted, mad that she couldn't have an epidural or anything else for pain. We offered as many non-medicinal comfort measures as we could, but her pain only got worse once her water was broken. Her amniotic fluid looked like thick pea soup. It was likely that her baby had been swimming in a pool of meconium for quite some time. The resident called Dr. Mather to give him an update on the patient's status and asked him to come to the hospital. Again, he said she'd be fine and he'd be there at 3:00 p.m. for delivery.

Prior to having her water broken, the baby's fetal heart rate had been reassuring, Category I—normal baseline, a reactive fetal heart rate with occasional variables. But, as soon as we broke her water, the fetal heart rate took a turn for the worse. Deep variables mirrored each contraction and the heartbeat sometimes dropped as low as 30 beats per minute, taking a full 60–90 seconds to return to baseline. This was coupled with variability that was minimal or even absent at times. Serena's baby was crying out to us, one beat at a time, communicating in his first language—the beat of his heart—that he was distressed and needed help.

The baby likely had the umbilical cord wrapped around his neck and an amnioinfusion could possibly help this situation. Amnioinfusion, infusing extra fluid into the uterus through an intrauterine pressure catheter (IUPC), can help cushion the umbilical cord and lessen fetal distress. Again, I called her doctor and asked if we could start this intervention and he said, "No, she's fine." I voiced my concern that I didn't think the baby was fine, the fetal heart rate was non-reassuring and that I thought he needed to come to the hospital. (This was before the days when doctors could see the fetal monitor strips in their offices.) Again, he said, "She's fine. I'll come at 3 o'clock."

I was scared and very concerned about this baby, who continued to have repetitive deep and wide variables. At 2:30 p.m., Serena was dilated to 9 cm. Other than supplemental oxygen for Serena, I didn't know what else to do, so the resident and I helped turn her onto her hands and knees to see if that position might alleviate the deep and wide fetal heart rate variables, all the while knowing that Dr. Mather hated the knee-chest position—"My patients aren't dogs and they don't belong in that position."

The next call was made by the charge nurse who called his office nurse and told her that Serena was ready to deliver and that he needed to come. His nurse told her that he was already on his way.

At that exact moment, Serena screamed the primal birthing scream that I'm pretty sure everyone on the unit could hear. Delivery was imminent. With only me and the resident present, the patient pushed once and delivered a screaming, vigorous boy. The umbilical cord was, in fact, tightly wrapped three times around his neck but he didn't seem to notice.

Within a minute of delivery, as we were moving Serena out of knee-chest position so that her placenta could be delivered, Dr. Mather came into the room—shocked that Serena had already delivered. He was furious that he missed it and yelled at the resident, "Don't you ever do that again. My patients aren't dogs!"

The resident started crying. Scared and intimidated, she told me later that she was concerned about how this incident might impact her residency. She apologized to him and vowed to him it would never happen again.

I was furious. Seething. The resident and I had not left Serena's side for almost two hours, doing everything we could within our scope of practice to help her and her baby. He is the one who taught me how to think critically, yet he didn't come when I called him.

I looked at him and said, "If you had come when I called you, you wouldn't have missed it!" He didn't say another word to me or anyone else in the room. Instead, he grabbed his jacket, walked out and went back to his office.

The next time I saw him, I asked if we could talk about what had happened, and he said, "No. I told you that baby would be fine and he is. We have nothing to talk about. I don't hold grudges."

We never talked about it again.

Chapter 10
"You Think You're So Smart"

Dr. Mather didn't induce labor very often, but when he did, he typically ordered one of two different methods of induction: RIP (Rupture membranes artificially, Internal monitors, Pitocin) or RIPE (Rupture membranes, Internal Monitors, Pitocin, Epidural). In each, the steps were to be followed in that order. He only induced patients who were already dilated. He rarely ordered cervical ripening.

I admitted Latrice early in my shift. She was being induced (RIPE was ordered) for her fifth baby. She had a history of such fast labors that they were afraid that if labor started on its own, she'd end up delivering her baby either at home or in her car.

Dr. Mather came by early to see Latrice. He broke her water and placed the internal monitors. He predicted a delivery time of 1:00 p.m. I started the Pitocin and before lunch, Latrice was uncomfortable and actively laboring. She got her epidural around noon but was still only dilated to 6 cm when Dr. Mather came to check on her during his lunch hour. He told me I was taking too long to get her delivered. He rolled his eyes, increased her Pitocin, smiled at me and left.

After frequent position changes and a good nap, Latrice felt some rectal pressure and told me, "This baby is coming!" I called Dr. Mather and finished setting the room up for delivery. When he got to her room, he joked that Latrice had ruined his afternoon office hours because she was an hour late having this baby. It was 2:00 p.m. after all—an hour later than he had predicted.

I was doing the last-minute room prep, getting everything ready to greet this baby. Dr. Mather looked at me, smiled and said, "You think you're so smart…why don't you put the gown on and deliver this baby? I'll stand here and see if I can figure out how to do your job." I thought he was joking until he said, "Go ahead, put that gown on so I can show you how things are done. It's going to happen to you at some point so you might as well know what you're doing."

It was as though he was finally communicating that he believed in and trusted me. I didn't hesitate to switch roles with him but I did ask Latrice if she was ok with this plan and she said, as she bore down involuntarily, "Sure. This'll be easy but you better hurry, this baby is coming now!"

By the time I quickly gowned and gloved, I could see the baby's head crowning. The doctor instructed Latrice when and how hard to push. She followed his directions perfectly and he guided me through the delivery as if this role reversal was something we had done together one hundred times before. Her baby boy came into the world easily and was wide-eyed and screaming as the doctor helped me place him on her belly. We clamped and cut the umbilical cord together and then he delivered the placenta.

He was right. I did end up delivering a handful of babies on my own throughout my career, most often in the bed, once on the bathroom floor. Babies come when they're ready. They don't care if we have gloves on or if there is a doctor in the room.

Dr. Mather had a profound impact on me, especially when I was a new Labor & Delivery nurse. I frequently chose to take care of his patients. He followed his intuition and was rarely wrong. It would almost be fair to say that he was never wrong, but I'm sure that can't be accurate. I watched him closely and marveled at his skill. Leading by example each time I worked with him, he taught me the importance of following my gut. I learned that listening to my intuition, which often came quicker than reflection, was also more precise.

I saw myself in him. I am strong-willed, opinionated and headstrong. We were both respected by our colleagues, and also feared at times (intimidation was never my intent). There is a shadow side of these strengths and I had to learn to acknowledge that as one of my greatest challenges. I had to temper my opinion and my expectations, and accept the reality that I was not always right. I needed to slow down and listen better. Thankfully, my growing awareness helped me inch forward as a better version of myself over the years. I became more confident following my intuition and softening my presence. I became better able to talk directly and assertively with my patients and my colleagues.

Chapter 11
Chain of Command

I was the charge nurse on a very busy Friday in October. I just wanted to get through the rest of my 12-hour shift so that I could go home, tuck my kids into bed and finish packing for the "adults-only" weekend we had planned with our close friends. The time we spent away from our children was brief and infrequent but essential for our mental health and life balance, therefore we treasured it. Being with our friends was easy and we enjoyed each other's company, no matter where we ventured. This reality bolstered me through this difficult shift.

It had been a day of relentless demand. Since the beginning of our shift at 7:00 a.m. 20+ babies had already been born—a mix of vaginal deliveries, scheduled and unscheduled C-sections, and two sets of twins. No one had a break of any sort. Finish with one patient, immediately get another.

At that time, our OB Triage was directly connected to the Labor & Delivery unit. At 5:30 p.m., I overheard one of the triage nurses on the telephone and it sounded as though she was arguing with someone. It had been an especially stressful day but this tone of voice was very out of character for her. I assumed something serious was unfolding.

Unbeknownst to me at that time, a new patient was being admitted to OB Triage. She had not been called in by a physician so her arrival came as a surprise. Lisa was 40 weeks pregnant and dilated to 6 cm, this was her first baby and she was in a lot of pain. The triage nurse assumed she was yet another active labor patient and gave her the last bed they had. One more patient to add to the long list of patients she had already admitted that day.

After obtaining a brief history and Lisa's vitals, the nurse attempted to find fetal heart tones. She was unsuccessful and asked the unit secretary to page the resident to come with a portable bedside ultrasound. I began to hear rumblings about Lisa once the resident had been paged.

The horrified wailing that came from Lisa's triage room told me that she had just been told that her baby did not have a heartbeat—her baby had died in-utero. It stopped me in my tracks—aware of my own need to calm down and take a deep breath, to put myself in Lisa's shoes instead of worrying about how I was going to manage yet another crisis on this day.

Lisa's nurse was once again on the phone, this time crying and visibly upset. She was no longer raising her voice, but simply stated, "I'll have you talk to Stephanie. She's in charge right now." She put the call on hold, waved me over and whispered, "Good luck!"

"Hello, this is Stephanie," I said, taking a deep breath to start the conversation. I felt so haggard.

"This is Dr. Madden. I just found out that Lisa accidentally came to your hospital instead of Eastern (a sister hospital three miles away). She needs to be transferred, by ambulance, to *my* hospital (Eastern) where *my* nurses can take care of *my* patient!"

My initial reaction, which I kept to myself, was, *You're kidding me, right?* Instead, I calmly explained the non-negotiable facts: "Even though she intended to deliver at your hospital, Lisa came here because it is closer to her home. She is actively laboring, very uncomfortable and tragically, her baby has passed away. She is begging for her epidural and does not want to be transferred. It would be unsafe to do so. She could deliver en route in the ambulance."

His response floored me. "I don't care. I want her transferred and I'll meet her there."

I reiterated that I would not transfer her. "She needs to stay here. If you cannot agree with me, I will go up the chain of command and connect you with the medical director of OB. You can discuss this with him." The phone went dead. He had hung up on me.

Before our shift ended, we helped Lisa deliver a beautiful, stillborn baby boy.

This caused an ugly parking-lot cry and I remember crying most of the drive home that night. A combination of utter fatigue, anger and disbelief. I loved my job but I was so exhausted.

I couldn't believe the shit I had to deal with sometimes.

I got home just in time to tuck my kids into bed and snuggle their freshly bathed bodies and sweet faces. I poured myself a glass of wine as my husband offered to make me something to eat.

I still had to pack.

For the first time that day, I sat down, resting my weary feet up on the ottoman. It was after 9:00 p.m. when our home landline phone rang. My husband answered, peeked his head around the corner and said, "There's some doctor on the phone for you."

I didn't want to talk anymore, especially about anything work related, but I took the call anyway.

"Stephanie, this is Dr. Madden. I'm sorry to bother you so late and at home."

"That's ok," I said.

He continued, "I just wanted to call you to apologize for my words and for treating you and the triage nurse so unprofessionally. I know Lisa well and was frustrated that I couldn't take care of her or be with her when she delivered. Thank you for standing up for her and making sure that decisions were made in her best interest."

Touched by his kind words, I started to cry again. I was keenly aware of my own vulnerability and my own strength. Thankful for this job that I love, despite the sometimes unreasonable, preposterous array of demands.

Chapter 12
Cradling the Cord

Julia, a short, petite woman, went into labor with her third baby on her actual due date, a cold wintery day in late February. Her first son was four years old and had been born vaginally after a long, slow labor and a couple hours of pushing. It was a "tight fit" and she had required low forceps to deliver him. Her second son made his debut quickly after a short, hard labor. Julia didn't know if she was carrying a boy or a girl this time. She believed that the natural gender reveal that happens at the time of the birth is one of the best surprises in life. It made up for all of the hard parts of pregnancy.

Julia was in labor when she got to the hospital around 2:00 in the afternoon. Contractions were painful but spread out. The nurse in OB Triage told her that while she was dilated to 5 cm, her baby's head was still "high" and had not settled in her cervix. She was transferred to a labor room where contractions continued, slow but steady. She was uncomfortable, yet still able to handle the pain.

By 5:00 p.m., she was getting more uncomfortable but was still only 6–7 cm dilated and the baby's head was still not engaged in her pelvis. *Must be another big baby*, I thought, as I cared for her. Her other boys had been almost 9 pounds each. She was frustrated and exhausted. She had hoped for an easy delivery like she'd had with her second baby. Since her bag of water couldn't be broken yet, she got her epidural and Pitocin was started to augment her labor while she took a much-needed nap.

At that same time, we started to see some early fetal heart rate variables on the monitor, likely caused by fetal head compression. When the baby's head is compressed during a contraction, the vagal response causes a slowing of the baby's heart rate. The dips in the baby's heart rate mirrored her contractions so we were hopeful that she was finally progressing in her labor. We repositioned her several times and she was able to rest comfortably. A very good epidural kept her from feeling any pain.

Knowing she was comfortable and because the early fetal heart rate variables had mostly resolved, I decided to take my dinner break. About ten minutes into my break, another nurse came into the break room and said, "Dr. Kramer just broke your patient's water."

I thought to myself, *That's not what I thought the plan was. She must be more dilated or the head must have come down some.* I looked up at the central monitor in the breakroom and saw that her baby was experiencing a prolonged fetal heart rate deceleration. The heart rate dipped down to the 60s and stayed there. I thought, *Perfect! Must be time to meet this baby.*

I abandoned my dinner and quickly went to her room. The baby's heart rate was still down. I told Julia that I needed to check her cervix quickly so that I could catch Dr.

Kramer before he got too far away from the unit. Third babies can come very quickly. Truthfully, I thought, *Either this baby's head is on the perineum and she is ready to deliver or we have a cord prolapse.* The baby had been so high in her pelvis that I wasn't sure which scenario I'd find.

I gloved up and put my hand in her vagina only to be greeted by a large loop of the baby's umbilical cord. I immediately pulled the call bell out of the wall with my other hand, to signal an emergency on the unit, and said to Julia, "I know this isn't what you want to hear but we need to do a C-section, right now."

She said, "I don't want to have a C-section!" As the room filled with staff to assist me, I calmly explained to her that we truly didn't have a choice. Because the baby's umbilical cord had come before the baby's head, a C-section was the only safe delivery option. She and her husband quickly agreed and we left for the operating room.

I rode on the bed with her, partially under her bedsheet, my hand cradling the cord while my fingers pushed the baby's head away from the cord. I could feel the baby's heartbeat (through the umbilical cord) in my hand the whole time.

This was not the first time that I had ridden down the hall, being whisked to the operating room, under a patient's sheet. I had a flashback to a different time I was on a patient's bed with a prolapsed cord in my hand. That patient was very calm and didn't appear upset at all; rather, she just had a perplexed look on her face. She furrowed her brow and said to me, "Do we have a problem here?"

That's when I realized that either we had not explained what was happening or it took her until that moment to grasp the seriousness of the situation. I said to her, "Yes, yes, we do have a problem here." Remembering that patient stopped my racing thoughts and brought me back to the present moment. Sometimes our minds play tricks during a crisis.

It all happened so quickly. The neonatal team was present and ready in the operating room. Because Julia had such a dense epidural, she did not need to go under general anesthesia and her husband Jesse was able to be present for the birth. Dr. Kramer quickly delivered a screaming, vigorous, unfazed, almost 9-pound baby boy.

The gender reveal wasn't the only surprise that happened that cold day in February.

In retrospect, I believe that this birth would have ended differently had her labor been managed more conservatively. The doctor knew that I questioned his decision to break her water. He kept making eye contact with me, as if pleading with me to protect him.

This beautiful baby boy did very well but this case bothered me for a long time. As a nurse, I have to accept that I am not in control of decisions regarding interventions and management of labor, especially when I'm on my dinner break.

Chapter 13
French Kiss

Tiffany, 19 years old, was being induced for her first baby. She was overweight, diabetic and covered in piercings and tattoos. I was told in report that no one was with her. The father of the baby was incarcerated.

When I first walked into her room, I smelled her before I saw her. The stench was that of a heavy smoker who hadn't showered and whose clothes were filthy. Her mouth was full of rotten and broken teeth and her breath reflected this. Rather than walk away from the foul smells, I offered to help her take a hot shower, wash her hair and brush her teeth before the induction was started. She was very gentle and sweet and so thankful for this fresh start to our day together.

It was midafternoon when the decision was made that we needed to try a different approach to managing Tiffany's labor. Pitocin had failed to get her into labor and we were concerned that her baby was probably TFTF (too fat to fit— this is not a standard medical acronym, rather a slang used to describe a big baby). Big babies are a common occurrence with moms who have poorly controlled diabetes.

The resident and I went into Tiffany's room to discuss the plan of care with her. A man was at her bedside whom I hadn't seen before. He was tall and toothpick-thin, heavily tattooed and bouncing off the walls. For the first time that day, Tiffany smiled as she introduced us to her boyfriend Joe. He had gotten out of jail, just in time to see his son born. He bragged that this was his sixth baby.

Our updated plan of care involved the resident breaking Tiffany's bag of water artificially to see if that would help her labor progress. To proceed, we had Tiffany lying on her back with her ankles together and her knees apart, the position most conducive to cervical exams and AROM (artificial rupture of membranes). Joe was sitting beside her, on the bed, which I thought was a bit unusual but I didn't say anything to him, nor did I ask him to move.

As the resident began to check Tiffany's cervix, Joe leaned over Tiffany and started to forcefully embrace and French-kiss her. He was clearly aroused by her position on the bed as his erection was impossible to miss through his baggy, filthy gray sweatpants. He appeared oblivious to everything else going on in the room and to how inappropriate his behavior was.

The resident and I exchanged glances, not sure what to say or how to proceed. It was like a scene from a low-budget B-movie.

The resident stopped what she was doing, covered Tiffany with a sheet and said, "Excuse me. This doesn't seem like the time or place for that." Tiffany started to squirm and Joe ignored us.

So, I said, "Joe, please stop kissing Tiffany right now. We are trying to break her water." Joe continued to ignore us and grope Tiffany. Finally, I walked around the bed and gently tapped his shoulder, which in retrospect, I realize I should not have done. He very angrily turned on me, furious about my intrusion. I firmly said, "Joe, please stop this."

He stood tall, looked down at me and said, "Why don't y'all get the f@%k on out of here!" Tiffany cowered on the bed, silent tears streaming down her face.

I put the call bell on and asked the charge nurse to call security immediately. Two security guards came quickly and escorted a fighting Joe from the room.

His penis was now flaccid but he was erect with rage, the likes of which I had never seen.

I had encountered angry and upset partners before that day. I had seen behavior that I deemed inappropriate. Two examples: one father walked naked around his girlfriend's hospital room as if he was staying in a motel and wasn't expecting any visitors. He became very angry when I told him he needed to get dressed. Or, the teenage boy who brought his entire video game PlayStation to the hospital. He was so mad when he realized it wasn't compatible with the hospital TV that he threw a temper tantrum. Sadly, I had also interacted with several men who bragged about the number of other children they had by other mothers, fifteen being the highest.

This was the first time that I was actually concerned for my own safety. I feared he might physically assault me, the resident, Tiffany or the security guards for that matter. Whether his rage was fueled by shame, or just by the fact that his entitled, sexual advances were thwarted, I'll never know. Thankfully, he never came back to the hospital.

I held Tiffany in my arms as she wept. She was scared, embarrassed, convinced that she had caused the entire scene, that it was all her fault. I did my best to convey to her that no one blamed her, that she was in no way responsible for Joe's behavior. She had done nothing wrong.

I hope that during poignant moments such as these, some of what I said sunk in, that Tiffany might be able to leave the hospital believing something different about herself and those who may harm her.

Chapter 14
Not a Dry Eye

It was a strangely quiet Saturday in April. Only a few labor patients that whole day. We had all eaten lunch and were sitting around the desk talking. I was the charge nurse.

Dr. Rowen came around the corner and said to me, "I just got a phone call from a patient but I didn't have any paper, so I couldn't write down her name. Anyway, her water broke, but she's not in labor yet. It's her third or fourth baby and she'll be coming in once she makes arrangements for her other kids. Let me know when she arrives and I'll come check her and get her admitted."

Easy enough. He left the unit and we resumed our conversation.

Roughly 30 minutes later, I got a phone call from the emergency room charge nurse telling me that an ambulance was 5 minutes out with a pregnant woman who had a cord dangling between her legs. He didn't know anything else about the patient (e.g., her name, her gestational age). More details would certainly have helped us prepare more efficiently for her arrival but this was before electronic patient medical records.

The OB resident and two nurses from our conversation circle quickly ran to the ER to meet the ambulance upon arrival. I went directly to the operating room with two other nurses to open up for a STAT C-section while the scrub tech went to scrub.

The surgical team was ready and the neonatal team was just arriving when a few minutes later, the patient (we still didn't know her name) was rolled into the operating room on a stretcher. She wore a pink flowered dress and her panties were around her ankles. She was alone and very scared, covered with an ambulance blanket. Once we transferred her to the OR table and the blanket was removed, we could see that, indeed, there was a cord prolapse. The resident's hand was simultaneously holding the umbilical cord and gently pushing the baby's head back, attempting to relieve pressure on the cord from the head.

While I started her IV, she tolerated the fusillade of questions from the physicians and anesthesiologist. Her first name was Mandy. She had no known medical allergies and this was her third baby. Shortly after her water broke, her parents had arrived to take care of her other two children. Her father was going to drive her to the hospital so that her husband, who was at work, could meet her there. Right before leaving for the hospital, she decided to empty her bladder one last time. It was then that, "the baby's cord was all of a sudden hanging between my legs." Her father immediately called 9–1–1.

The umbilical cord looked to be full-term size but we were not able to ascertain her actual due date, which might have given us more insight on what to anticipate with the baby. Best we could estimate, the umbilical cord—the baby's lifeline—had been prolapsed for between 30–45 minutes. It's not only the length of time a cord is prolapsed that is threatening, it's the amount of time the cord is compressed that matters. When the cord is compressed, the baby's supply of oxygen is diminished, causing potential brain damage or death. We all knew that the likelihood that this baby would be born alive was very slim since no attempt had been made to relieve pressure on the cord prior to Mandy's arrival in the ER.

About five minutes passed between when Mandy was rolled into the operating room, her IV started, she was put under general anesthesia and underwent an emergency C-section. In those stressful, chaotic five minutes, we did not attempt to find fetal heart tones. Taking the time to do that would not have changed our course of action because every second mattered. After Mandy was under general anesthesia, Dr. Rowen walked into the operating room to see if he could assist the teams with anything. "Hmmm," he said, "I wonder if this is my patient. The one who called to tell me that her water broke." Mandy was his patient.

Roughly one minute later, a screaming, vigorous full-term baby girl was delivered. A medical miracle for which the whole team cheered. There was not a dry eye in the operating room.

I never expected to hear this baby cry, or for her to be vigorous, alive and well. It appeared as though she suffered no ill effects from the protracted cord prolapse. Every staff person in the OR, myself included, either cheered with excitement or cried tears of relief.

It all happened so quickly. When her husband was brought to the recovery room, he was so baffled by the string of events that he had completely missed. He cried quietly as he shook his head, trying to take in our explanation. The neonatologist handed him his beautiful daughter, her eyes wide open and her dark hair peeking out from under the baby hat. His wife, groggy from the anesthesia and painful from the surgery, was also trying her best to make sense of what had just happened to her. She was still wearing the pink dress she had worn as she made pancakes for her family that morning.

This day was pivotal for me. I felt that for the first time, I was able to fully embrace the fact that coming to work each day as a Labor & Delivery nurse was like agreeing to ride on an emotional rollercoaster for twelve hours. The heights of unexpected joy, followed by the lows of tragedy. Baffled confusion and shock, followed by the balm of good fortune. Not all that different from real life outside the hospital.

Chapter 15
HIV

The year was 1981. I was 16 years old, visiting my dad, who lived in Houston, Texas, at the time. While he was working, I spent long lazy days lounging by the pool, slathered up with Hawaiian Tropic dark tanning oil, reading scary Stephen King novels and listening to the radio.

The DJ was spinning all of my favorite pop rock tunes—"Bette Davis Eyes", "Lady", "Endless Love", etc. I was reading my book and about to doze off when the DJ started talking about HIV and AIDS, this new "Gay Disease" that was killing "tons of gay men". (These exact words of his have always stuck with me.)

This was all new to me and it fully captured my attention. I did not nap. The virus had been identified as Human Immunodeficiency Virus (HIV). The associated syndrome that was claiming so many lives was called Acquired Immune Deficiency Syndrome (AIDS). This would escalate into a worldwide public health emergency.

Fast forward to 2001. A married woman in her early 30s delivered her third baby in a small, rural hospital seemingly without incident. Everything appeared to go as it should.

Three weeks later, she returned to the emergency room of that same rural hospital with her baby girl, who had become gravely ill, ostensibly overnight. Her daughter was lethargic, no longer breastfeeding, had constant diarrhea and a high fever. She was diagnosed with pneumonia and transferred to the Intensive Care Unit (ICU) of our nearby children's hospital.

During the course of the baby's hospital stay, multiple blood tests were run, hoping to find an answer as to why she was so sick and not responding to any of the treatment and care provided to her. Shockingly, one of her blood tests came back showing that she was HIV positive. She was clearly dying of AIDS. There was nothing else that could be done for her so she was kept comfortable by a compassionate palliative care team, until her death one week later.

The mother was devastated and completely caught off-guard by this diagnosis. How could her daughter have HIV/AIDS? She was a married, straight woman in a monogamous relationship. There must be some mistake. Shortly after their daughter's death, her husband confessed to her that he was a closeted gay man who had had multiple affairs with men, often involving unprotected sexual relations. He knew he was HIV positive and had never told her. After being tested herself, she learned that she was also HIV positive and had inadvertently passed along the virus to their daughter. Tragically, AIDS claimed this woman's life less than a year later. This was considered a sentinel event, as both deaths were wholly unexpected.

Fast forward to 2005. Since 1995, Center for Disease Control has recommended all pregnant women be tested for HIV and, if found to be infected, they should be offered treatment for themselves to improve their health and to help prevent passing the virus to their infant (Centers for Disease Control and Prevention, n.d.).

However, even though testing pregnant women during their prenatal course for HIV was available, it was strictly voluntary and often declined. In fact, one doctor's office naively said, "I don't have that patient population in my office."

It is because of cases like the one described above that pregnant women are now tested for HIV early in their pregnancy, as part of the routine prenatal labs. Testing in some clinics and offices is repeated two more times throughout the pregnancy, once in each of the second and third trimester. Patients can refuse to have the test done, but their baby will be tested upon birth, per protocol order of the pediatrician.

Thankfully, so much more is known now about the transmission and treatment of HIV and AIDS than back in the 1980's, and even more since the early 2000's. In addition to testing protocols, there are antiviral medications and delivery practices adapted to help prevent transmission of HIV from a mother to her infant, if it is known that the HIV virus is present, ahead of delivery.

Chapter 16
The Sound of Silence

Kara was in her early thirties, married, with an active toddler at home. She came into my care when she was 30 weeks pregnant with her second child, a baby boy who had passed away in-utero.

She and Henry had known from early ultrasounds that the outcome of this pregnancy would be grave. Their baby had Cystic Hygroma and Fetal Hydrops. This meant that there were several cysts around his neck area and extra fluid had accumulated under his skin, like balloons filled with too much water. Kara told me that she and Henry had done extensive research and had decided that based on what they had read and pictures they had seen, they did not wish to see, touch or hold their son. They were afraid to even catch a glimpse of what he looked like and requested that I take him from the room immediately after he was born.

I sat with them for a long time, listening to them talk of their profound fears, their heart-wrenching sadness, their love for their daughter at home and their thankfulness that their unborn son would never suffer any pain brought on by his congenital anomalies. I talked with them about the stages of grief, a process that is different for each person, each marriage, each family member and each friend.

I encouraged them to do what they thought was unfathomable: to look at, touch and hold their baby after he was born, even if only for a short while. I hoped that this brave act would help them in their grieving process. I reassured them that babies usually don't look as disfigured or scary as we are told they will. After some time for reflection, and after speaking with the bereavement counselor, who also encouraged them to spend time with their son, they decided to at least "give it a try".

Later that afternoon, their son was born. The cysts that had started near his neck had spread like a lion's mane around his face, but because his eyes and nose were clearly visible, this made him appear angelic. His skin was taut with fluid. Several of the blisters that covered his body had split open and oozed a yellowish fluid when they were touched.

Julia and Henry held, touched, kissed, named, took photos of their son and cried into his broken skin. I was reminded of the unconditional love that streams forth when we see and hold our babies for the first time, regardless of how they look. They belong to us. They are part of us. They are our babies, even when they are randomly marred by ruthless, lethal anomalies. They are seen by us with loving eyes and grieving hearts.

At the birth of a new baby, whether vaginally or by C-section, the sound of that first cry is one that brings about the most collective and deep sighs of relief from parents, staff and family or friends present in the room. That first cry tells us our baby is alive. That cry also tells us that our newborns are not terribly happy about the vast changes that have just taken place in their world. Their instinctive response in this moment is an understandable reaction to this transition and all that their senses are experiencing: bright lights, cold air, physical touch, skin to skin, warm blankets, the sounds of people and equipment, the smell of perfume and cautery, the taste of sugar water and colostrum (known as "liquid gold", nature's precursor to breast milk).

In stark contrast, when our babies pass away before they are born, there is an astonishing absence of that cry. Stillborn babies are silent, still and motionless. Often, their eyes are open. Sometimes, they are visually perfect; other times, there are anomalies so profound that this can cause the parents to shudder reflexively and have nightmares for years to come (a bereaved mother once told me this).

One of the most important roles of the Labor & Delivery nurse is to educate patients about the birthing process and to teach them what to expect throughout. For my patients who would be delivering a stillborn baby, that meant gently preparing them for the sound of silence that was to come. The quietness after the birth of a stillborn baby is deafening, especially if the patient has had other children and can recall the cry, the sounds and the early interactions with that new baby's life.

Chapter 17
Postpartum Psychosis

Jackie had a very complicated pregnancy history. According to her husband, Steve, her first pregnancy was "A beautiful experience. She loved being pregnant!" Her first labor and delivery experience, however, was anything but beautiful. "It was very traumatic," Steve told me. "She had labored for 48 hours, pushed for more than three hours and ultimately ended up with an emergency C-section."

Following the birth of her first daughter, Jackie suffered from severe clinical postpartum depression, which escalated quickly to postpartum psychosis. She experienced an abrupt onset of psychotic-like symptoms which included delusions and some hallucinations. Her speech was incoherent, and she couldn't sleep. She became fixated on suicide and after coming up with a detailed plan of how she would kill herself, she decided that she must first smother her daughter, "to put her out of her own misery. I am the worst mother ever and she deserves so much better."

Thankfully, during a rare, lucid moment, she shared these fantasies with Steve. He was able to take his daughter to his parents and facilitate Jackie's immediate hospitalization at a local mental health hospital where she would be kept safe, under constant supervision. She was started on several medications. She was discharged 14 days later and continued to stabilize on her medications/treatment plan. She was reunited with her daughter. She joined a postpartum depression support group and was able to take care of herself and her daughter.

When Jackie was pregnant with their second daughter two years later, she decided to have a home birth with a lay midwife. She was convinced that her postpartum psychosis was a direct result of the trauma she experienced with her first birth. She believed that if she could just have a normal vaginal delivery at home, all would be well.

When the time came, her second labor progressed normally, at home, with her supportive, lay midwife. She started pushing. She pushed. And pushed. And pushed. After four hours, she was exhausted and her midwife suggested that they go to the hospital to be evaluated. She ended up with a repeat emergency C-section, and in her mind, she had failed again.

For her third pregnancy, Jackie decided to deliver in the hospital but was so determined to try and have this baby vaginally that she refused to schedule a repeat C-section. She was going to wait until labor started naturally.

One day past her due date with her third baby, she went to her routine doctor's appointment, knowing that because she was overdue, the main topic of discussion would be her delivery options. She knew that she hadn't yet felt any contractions or early signs of labor but she was still hopeful that the third time would be the charm.

Shockingly, her doctor couldn't find the baby's heartbeat during her office visit. This was confirmed by a bedside ultrasound. Her unborn baby had died, for no apparent reason.

She allowed her doctor to schedule a repeat C-section for that afternoon. That's when I met her. Jackie was barely able to speak or make eye contact with me. She was reticent, bordering on catatonic. Her husband is the one who shared her heartbreaking story with me. To ensure her safety, we developed a plan with Steve to have a sitter (a hospital staff care provider who would never leave her side) throughout her entire hospital stay. Once discharged, she would again go to the local mental health hospital for intensive, inpatient care.

This story was difficult for me to write because Jackie spoke virtually no words to me. All of this information came from her terribly distressed yet fully supportive, proactive husband. He was heavily burdened with the reality of his wife's dire mental state and the unbelievable death of his third daughter.

For her, I imagine the heartache was just too heavy a burden to carry and her soul was looking for a way to survive. I pray that Jackie and Steve, and all other grieving parents, get the help and support that they need.

Chapter 18
Hardened to Everything

Tabitha was 29 years old and pregnant for the 12th time. When she came to Labor & Delivery, she was 35 weeks pregnant. She was coming down from OB Special Care to have a C-section, her first. Of her previous 11 pregnancies, only two had been vaginal deliveries. The other nine had been miscarriages or abortions. She did not have custody of her two sons, ages 6 and 10; they were both in foster care and she knew nothing about how they were doing or where they lived.

Tabitha was addicted to heroin, cocaine, methadone and alcohol. She smoked two packs of cigarettes a day and spoke openly of her substance abuse and drug dependence. She was homeless and frequently exchanged sex for housing and drugs. She was not certain, but she thought the father of her baby was a man who raped her after she refused a "sex for housing" arrangement. He was incarcerated for unrelated drug charges. She never reported the rape. She thought no one would believe her.

While caring for her, Tabitha told me that six weeks prior, she had been gangraped, nearly overdosed and was brought to the hospital. I was told by another nurse, who had cared for her during this prior admission, that when she was awake, she alternated between sobbing "I want my mommy" and cursing loudly in every sentence and/or behaving violently toward staff members. She refused to eat, threw aside her cordless baby monitors and took off down the hall, leaving the hospital against medical advice. I surmised the mommy she cried for was the mommy she still yearned for.

Tabitha's body was covered in cheap, poorly done tattoos. Literally every square inch of her body, except the bottoms of her feet and the palms of her hands, were covered in them. She was malnourished and dreadfully underweight. Her teeth were rotten and broken. Her hair looked like it hadn't been washed in weeks. Tabitha existed in the margins, with nobody to watch out for or care for her.

An ultrasound done at her bedside that morning on OB Special Care showed that there was no amniotic fluid around her baby. Nothing protecting him in her uterus. His fetal heart tracing showed that he was in distress and had no reserve. It was essential that the baby be delivered, and because we knew he would not tolerate an induction of labor, we needed to do a C-section.

Connecting with Tabitha and establishing a rapport with her was imperative if I was going to care for her in the ways that she needed. It took several minutes of me being alone in the room with her before she would even look at me. When she realized I wasn't going to leave her or judge her, she started to open up and tell me her story. Lots of swear words, all without tears. She had no desire for rehab and refused all offers of help. She agreed to the cesarean section but refused to have her tubes tied.

Immediately after her son was born, he went to the neonatal intensive care unit (NICU) and ultimately, he would be placed directly in foster care. Tabitha never looked at him or asked anything about him. She appeared to have no interest in him, solidified by the fact that she refused to visit him in the NICU. All she wanted was narcotics for her pain, which we were never able to get under control.

This was the only time during my career that I saw complete and utter rejection of one's baby. Even the coldest woman often melts a tiny bit when her baby is born. Tabitha seemed hardened to it all. This precious new life went ignored by her. It haunts me to think of all that may have happened in her life to leave her so lost and alone. I speculate that her inability to receive and nurture her own baby was proportionate to the rejection, neglect and abuse she experienced as a child. I think of her often. I wonder where she is and if she is still living.

We all need to be loved.

Chapter 19
A Smell Like No Other

Chorioamnionitis (referred to as chorio) is a very serious infection involving the amniotic fluid and membranes that surround the baby in-utero. The causes vary, but the infection can begin in the woman's vagina, rectum or anus and spread up to the uterus, infecting the fluid, the placenta and ultimately the baby. Signs and symptoms of chorio often include fever, a tender or painful abdomen and foul-smelling vaginal discharge.

Monica was a beautiful, 28-year-old woman who came to the hospital in active labor. She was full term, very uncomfortable and lovingly supported by her husband, Jeff. This was her first pregnancy, and it had been uncomplicated. She was healthy with no risk factors. In OB Triage, the nurse found Monica dilated to 7 cm with a bulging bag of water. She was having frequent contractions and rated her pain as a 10/10 on the pain scale. She was quietly clinging to Jeff, begging for pain relief and hoping she wasn't too late for her epidural.

Concern quickly developed when the triage nurse discovered that Monica had a fever of 103.6 degrees and that her baby's heart rate was 180 bpm (beats per minute). Normal is 110–160 bpm. Between contractions, Monica shared that earlier in the day, she had experienced an unusual backache. She also reported that she felt more fatigue than normal. In a quiet voice, she attributed it to the fact that, "I'm very pregnant and so ready to meet this baby!"

Jeff grinned and softly added, "We can't wait to actually call this baby by his or her name instead of 'it'. Either Nathan or Kimberly."

Monica was transferred to a labor room where I took over her care. We weren't sure yet as to the cause of her fever but nevertheless, we started IV antibiotics and called anesthesia for her epidural. She now rated her pain as a 20/10. She was tearful, miserable, still clinging to Jeff and pleading for relief from the relentless pain. She was remarkably calm, able to speak only in a hushed, woeful voice.

Ten minutes later, she got her epidural. She was in the transition phase of labor so unfortunately, she only obtained partial pain relief and continued to rate her pain as 10/10. Also, even though she had been given Extra Strength Tylenol in OB Triage, her fever had only come down to 101 degrees and the baby's heart rate continued running 170–180 bpm. Monica's contractions were coming every 1–2 minutes with very little break in-between. Then, the baby started to have repetitive late decelerations, an ominous sign of fetal distress.

We were all very concerned. No question, we had a stressful, urgent situation on our hands: Monica's pain was uncontrollable (despite the epidural), her fever was creeping back up and her baby was showing significant signs of distress. A cervical exam showed that Monica's labor had stalled at 8 cm. She was not even close to a vaginal birth and time was of the essence. The decision was made to do STAT C-section under general anesthesia. Monica and Jeff were both in agreement. We moved quickly to the operating room, leaving Jeff behind—stunned, scared and tearful.

General anesthesia was induced and the neonatal team was present and ready to accept the baby. Everyone in the operating room presumed Monica had chorioamnionitis—but even when you're ready for it, you can never be fully prepared for the putrid smell that permeates the room once the infected patient's uterus is opened and the bag of water is broken.

I was 15 feet away from the OR table but the stench pierced my nostrils, right through my surgical mask. I gagged and was instantly nauseous. A similar response rippled through the operating room—heads shaking, bodies quivering—everyone simultaneously unsettled by it. The amniotic fluid looked like rancid pea soup. The limp, unresponsive baby girl's skin was stained by meconium and looked yellowish-green. Her full head of black hair looked like it had been dyed a horrendous shade of brownish green. She needed full resuscitation and was transferred quickly to the NICU.

Two days later, I visited Monica on the postpartum floor to see how she and her daughter Kimberly were doing. Kimberly remained in the NICU but was "doing pretty well, all things considered." Monica and Kimberly had both tested positive for Group B Beta Strep and were being treated with antibiotics. Monica and Jeff were humbly grateful for the care that they received, even though the birth had not happened anything like they had imagined it would.

Chapter 20
Drenched with Sweat

Maria was a 35-year-old, married woman who came to the hospital in active labor with her sixth baby. Her first five children were all normal vaginal deliveries without any complications and she had no significant health or social history. Her only risk factor was her age.

When her water broke spontaneously, she was dilated to 8 cm but the baby was still quite high, not yet engaged in her pelvis. Considering she had been through this five times before, her labor was taking longer than anyone expected. She decided to get an epidural to see if relaxing and sleeping would help this baby make his appearance.

It is standard protocol after an epidural for a nurse to remain in the patient's room for 20 minutes—making sure that the procedure is tolerated, that pain relief is obtained and that there isn't any significant drop in maternal blood pressure. It was within that first 20 minutes that Maria reported feeling nauseated. Within seconds, her eyes rolled back in her head and she started foaming at the mouth. It looked like she was having a seizure.

The nurse pressed the call bell immediately and asked for the attending physician, who promptly came to the room. It wasn't long after that Maria stopped breathing and went into respiratory arrest. The anesthesiologist who had just placed the epidural was called STAT to the room and the obstetrician called an emergency C-section. The patient was bagged per the anesthesiologist and transferred immediately to the operating room.

It was at about this time that the team suspected an amniotic fluid embolism—a true life-threatening obstetric emergency responsible for 7.5–10% of maternal mortality during labor in the United States.

Further complicating matters, as Maria was intubated and put under general anesthesia for her cesarean, she went into cardiac arrest (her heart stopped beating). Chest compressions were started while her abdomen was being prepped and continued while the C-section was performed. Her baby boy was quickly delivered and handed to the neonatal team. He needed full resuscitation and was immediately transferred to the NICU.

Maria's uterus was repaired at the conclusion of her cesarean, but by the time the surgeons were ready to close her abdomen, she was experiencing full-blown disseminated intravascular coagulation (DIC). Her blood looked like Kool-Aid—thin and no longer able to clot properly. An ominous sign. A massive transfusion protocol was initiated and it was painfully clear that we were fighting to save Maria's life.

Blood was everywhere. The foreheads and backs of everyone in the operating room were drenched with sweat. The clock was the enemy. The longer it took to get her bleeding under control, the less likely she was to survive. The ICU trauma team joined our fight and the decision was made to do a hysterectomy. Once her uterus was removed, she was transferred to the surgical intensive care unit (SICU) in very critical condition. We had just spent four grueling hours in the operating room—administering over 100 units of blood and blood products, countless medications and lab draws to save her life.

Just four days later, we went to visit Maria and her newborn son. She had made a remarkable recovery and had been transferred from the ICU to a regular postpartum room and her son was out of the NICU. Her primary nurse was with me, the same nurse who had performed the chest compressions, and she said to Maria, "It's so nice to see you. I'm SO glad you are doing ok!"

Maria sweetly responded, "Me and my baby were never in real danger."

Amniotic Fluid Embolism (AFE), a life-threatening obstetric crisis, happens roughly one time in every 40,000 deliveries. This was the first case of AFE I was ever involved with, almost 20 years into my career as a Labor & Delivery nurse. I knew about them and had heard of them happening on our unit, but surprisingly, none had ever happened during my shift or under my care.

I was just finishing my regular 8-hour shift. I was walking out of our recovery room when I heard the STAT overhead page that a cardiac arrest code was happening in our operating room. This was highly unusual and at first, I wondered if a mistake had been made by the hospital operator. Or a staff member had accidentally pushed the code button. Everyone is human and mistakes like this can happen.

Since I was on my way home, I decided to swing into the operating room just to check that everything was ok. It took me a few seconds to actually register and believe what my eyes were seeing. I had arrived just prior to the hospital code team. The nurse was on the OR table doing chest compressions as the baby was being delivered. I had never seen such a thing.

Every single minute, spanning the four long hours we fought to save Maria's life, both dragged and flew by. There was always something to be done: running for supplies, paging a different doctor or chief resident, running to blood bank for more blood products (of which we almost bled them dry-no pun intended), ordering lab work and facilitating transfer of blood vials to the lab, all while documenting the time and dose of each medication, each blood product, each intervention, each equipment charge, each physician notification...all to be documented in Maria's electronic medical record later, once Maria left our care. In this case, work first—chart later.

Maria was transferred to the surgical ICU at 7:15 that evening. Unstable. Yet alive. The 4 nurses involved in her care, myself included in that number, spent the next 1.5 hours making sure that our documentation reflected all that we had done to manage this crisis and help save Maria's life.

We left the hospital together and went to a local brewpub for dinner and drinks. We celebrated the fact that Maria was still alive when we left the hospital and that the bond of our work family ran so deep. These close relationships filled my soul and kept me going, especially since we relied so heavily upon each other to navigate the stress during a crisis, as we had just done for the last 5 grueling hours.

Chapter 21
What Happens in Vegas

Emily was a 40-year-old virgin. She had been single her whole life and had never had a serious boyfriend. She decided she was sick of her current reality, so she went shopping for some new clothes and bought a plane ticket for a trip to Las Vegas with her best friend. They wanted to see what it was like to "hit the town". In her words, "Maybe we could even get laid. Because, honestly, what happens in Vegas, stays in Vegas." (She was quite funny and very open about her story.)

Once in Vegas, Emily and her girlfriend got dressed up and hit the town. They enjoyed a nice dinner and then stumbled upon a trendy, crowded nightclub where they danced and played the scene. They found men to spend the evening with—including, as they had hoped, "getting laid".

They flew home together two days later. No regrets. Spent money they didn't have, but the laughter, food, music, dancing and energy they experienced were worth every penny. Little did Emily know at the time, she was pregnant. Her bestie was not.

When I met Emily, she was in labor. I was with her when she easily delivered her beautiful daughter. She eagerly shared her Vegas story with me and acknowledged that she had always loved children. She was a kindergarten teacher and had given up the hope that she would ever get to be a mother. She certainly hadn't planned to be a single parent but with the help of her loving, supportive family, she and her daughter would become a dynamic duo.

Throughout my career, I saw many definitions of the word "family". Married, straight, lesbian, bisexual and non-binary, single women involved with the father of the baby (FOB), single not involved with the FOB, etc.

*What I learned to appreciate through the years was that it's not **who** the family unit is made of, but rather **what** the family relationships consist of: respect, connection, commitment, trust, honesty, kindness, the ability to navigate conflict. These characteristics are the foundation of a stable family life, which is ultimately what matters most when bringing a new baby home.*

Chapter 22
Steadfast (In Her) Refusal

Salma was a 36-year-old, married, petite African immigrant. She came to the hospital early one morning after laboring for several hours at home. She was completely dilated, in a great deal of pain and desperately trying to push her baby out.

This was her third baby. Her two sons were both born by C-section (in the USA) after she attempted unsuccessfully to deliver them vaginally. We knew that her chance of a successful vaginal birth after cesarean (VBAC) was slim, especially after two prior cesareans. To complicate matters, Salma and her husband spoke only Swahili. They did not speak or understand any English. Language barriers are never easy, and in difficult cases like these, it's like climbing up a mountainside through thick mud. Accessing an interpreter was difficult and took extra time because the specific dialect they spoke was uncommon and rarely used. Ultimately, we were able to arrange a virtual interpreter through our iPad, but the connection was spotty at best.

When the fetal monitor was applied, we discovered that Salma's baby was in serious distress, with Category III fetal heart tones. There is no Category IV. This baby needed to be delivered immediately. After watching Salma push and realizing that no progress was being made toward a vaginal delivery, the physician determined a STAT C-section was necessary. Between screams and pushing with contractions, the interpreter communicated this to Salma and her husband. Salma refused the cesarean and continued to push hard with each contraction. We were watching her baby's heart tones, standing by helplessly while she pushed, knowing her baby was dying on the monitor. We tried everything we could to help her push and she continued to refuse the cesarean, any blood draws or an IV. Everything we offered her, she adamantly refused. Her husband sat in a chair in the corner, head in his hands, shaking his head.

Roughly an hour after her arrival on the unit, the baby's heart tones on the monitor showed a perfectly straight, downward spiraling line. Salma's baby's heartbeat had dropped to 40 beats per minute. Salma and her husband were told that their baby was actively dying and she continued to refuse the cesarean. Her husband was crying, visibly scared and finally suggested to Salma that she should consent to a cesarean delivery. Seeing her husband's distress, Salma reluctantly agreed instead to the use of forceps to assist in the delivery of her baby. Forceps were applied and Salma's screams were heard throughout the entire Labor & Delivery floor until the moment her daughter was born, vaginally.

Salma's daughter looked dead when she was born and was immediately handed to the waiting neonatal team. Her

Apgar scores were 0-0-0-0-1, which means it took the neonatal team 20 minutes to get her heart beating again.

The first vaginal birth that Salma was able to experience was one that ended in tragedy.

The baby lived in the NICU for over a month. She was able to breathe on her own but required a feeding tube for her nutrition. The NICU team encouraged Salma to take the baby home with hospice but she refused. The baby eventually passed away in the NICU.

In Africa, cesarean sections are often associated with maternal death, and sadly, babies frequently die there. From Salma's perspective, her life needed to be saved first so that she could care for her other children at home. She told the pastoral team in NICU that she believed she would always just have more children.

This was a very traumatic birth to be part of. I initially struggled with feeling so much anger toward her. It is impossible to imagine how difficult this must have been for Salma and her husband. I didn't know what was happening inside Salma's brain for two poignant reasons: the language barrier and the urgency of the moment. At the time of the delivery, it seemed as though she was letting her baby die so she could have a vaginal delivery. I feel ashamed of my anger now as I don't believe that was the case for her at all. She was steadfast in her refusal because she simply wanted to stay alive for her family and was so afraid that she would die if she consented to another C-section.

I learned so much through the years regarding culture and context, of my own ethnocentricity—how some patients and their families didn't fit into my narrow view of what I thought was "right" or "normal". It doesn't mean that I had to like or agree with all things as a delivery nurse, it just meant that when I learned to understand the culture, context, and meaning behind their decision-making, it helped me be more compassionate, accepting, and a much better bedside nurse.

Chapter 23
We Just Played Together

It was a very busy day and the C-section schedule was full. I had signed up to be the baby nurse (the nurse focused on caring for the baby in the operating room) for our 1:30 p.m. case. I was excited to be paired with one of my favorite co-workers, which always helped make a busy day better. Reviewing the patients' chart prior to her arrival, we knew that she was high-risk and being cared for by our Maternal Fetal Medicine (MFM) group.

Sharon was 36 years old. She was morbidly obese with a BMI (Body Mass Index) of 65. (Between 18.5 and 24.9 is considered normal. Some hospitals can't safely care for patients with a BMI of 65 due to equipment and bed concerns.) She had chronic hypertension (high blood pressure) and suffered from homozygous factor V Leiden, meaning that she had an increased risk of forming abnormal or harmful blood clots. She also had a history of a blood clot (deep vein thrombosis or DVT) in her right leg and had two prior C-sections. Her daughters were 15 and 2.

Sharon was referred to our MFM team for her delivery, but her pregnancy had been managed by a family practice physician in the small town where she lived. Due to her blood clot history, she had been on Lovenox, then Heparin (blood thinners used to prevent and treat blood clots) prior to admission, having stopped the Heparin as ordered, the day prior to her scheduled repeat C-section.

I was eating lunch when Sharon arrived on the unit, and my co-worker began getting her prepped for surgery. Part of that process includes obtaining a 20-minute fetal monitor strip, which is standard practice for all of our patients who are scheduled for a C-section. This can be a difficult task when the patient is morbidly obese.

After spending approximately 15 minutes (unsuccessfully) trying to find fetal heart tones, my colleague called out of the patient's room and asked the resident to come in with the ultrasound machine to try and find the baby's heartbeat. At this point, Sharon did not realize there was a problem. Using the bedside ultrasound, the resident discovered that there was no fetal movement or fetal heart motion. The attending physician was called to the room and confirmed our fears. This baby, her first boy, had passed away in-utero and she still had no idea.

The physician held Sharon's hand and gently said, "I'm so sorry to tell you that your son does not have a heartbeat. He has passed away."

Sharon's husband Roger and her sister Chris were in the room. Roger was sleeping in a chair with his head against the wall, alternating between snoring loudly and apneic episodes. His baseball cap rested sideways on his head. Chris was sitting with Sharon. Sporting bleached blonde hair, she wore a bright pink velour tank top and shorts. The tattoo on her right shoulder, a Road Runner kissing a big heart, had her initials in it. We later learned that she was diabetic and had lost one of her own babies at 6 months gestation.

The gentle announcement of the baby's death brought on a guttural scream from Sharon that echoed through the room and hallway, sending shockwaves through our hearts and souls. (Unfortunately, this is a familiar sound to all Labor & Delivery nurses. There is no cry more heart-wrenching.) Her shriek startled Roger awake, who up until now, was unaware of his son's death. He stumbled to Sharon's side, wide-eyed and confused. They were here to have a son, how could this possibly be happening?

As Sharon cried, she said, "I told them to deliver me two weeks ago and they didn't listen to me."

Through tears, Chris said, "But we just played together yesterday. He was kicking and moving around like crazy!"

We offered the family time to grasp the situation and begin their grief before we proceeded with the cesarean. We were obligated to talk about her options and briefly discussed inducing labor and attempting a trial of labor after cesarean (TOLAC) but everyone in the room knew that the likelihood of that being successful, with Sharon's risk factors and history, was slim to none.

When Denny (named after their favorite race-car driver) was delivered stillborn, the operating room was silent. He weighed 10#14oz. There was no obvious cause of death. Thick yellowish-green meconium, the texture of pea soup, coated his peeling and blistered skin. This skin condition indicated that his death had likely occurred long before the 24 hours prior to his birth, when they thought they had "played together".

I was touched by their collective, raw agony. Despite their shock and utter disbelief, they cradled their precious son and took a lot of pictures. When I offered to wash the baby's hair so they could take some of it home with them, they were surprised that this was an option for them. They were so grateful for this memento and all the others that we made for them (i.e., footprints, a plaster of Paris mold of his hands and feet, a Christmas tree ornament with his name and birthdate). This was how I tried, with my actions, to convey my deepest sympathies to them. I wanted them to know how much I cared for them in the tragic, unexpected loss of their son.

Chapter 24
High Touch-Low Tech

It was 2:35 p.m. and I had just transferred my second scheduled cesarean patient of the day to the postpartum floor. I was scheduled to work until 3:00 p.m. and was really looking forward to meeting a girlfriend at 4:00 for yoga after work. The unit had been pretty busy that day but I had taken a lunch break and it looked like I would get out on time.

My co-worker and I came around the corner from dropping off our patient to check in with our charge nurse. She looked at us both and said, "Please don't hate me but there are two patients in OB Triage who need to come up now. One is completely dilated, wants the High Touch-Low Tech (HTLT) room and plans to be delivered by a midwife. The other is dilated 4–5 cm and wants her epidural." *As I progressed in my career, it became clear to me that I preferred the operating room. The all-natural, no-intervention childbirth option 25 minutes before the end of my shift...not my first choice but I took it anyway.*

Our unit had two HTLT rooms and before that day, I had never set foot in them. There is a core group of nurses specially trained to work with this patient population and I chose not to be one of them. As such, I didn't know where the small number of supplies were kept. There was no fetal monitor. Instead, handheld dopplers were used to auscultate fetal heart tones every 15 minutes on healthy risk-free mothers. There are no IV supplies or blood pressure cuffs and the queen-size bed doesn't break apart or move around. These rooms are the closest you can come to a home birth while still delivering in the hospital.

I went down to pick up Crystal, the completely dilated patient who was planning on an all-natural birth. I met her, her midwife and her doula in the hallway. Crystal was deeply focused, headphones on. She executed total control of herself and her labor pain. Brenda, her doula (a trained professional who helps support the birthing family), was quietly supportive and also pushing the stretcher. Crystal's husband Brad was on his way to the hospital from work.

Crystal was 40 weeks pregnant, ready to deliver her second baby on her due date. Her two-year-old daughter had also been born on her due date, a coincidence twice over that doesn't happen very often. I quietly suggested, between contractions, that perhaps they should play the lottery with the birth dates as numbers and Crystal actually smiled at me, despite her intense concentration.

Five minutes after we got to the birthing room, Brad arrived, anxious that he may have missed the birth. Right after him, the photographer, hired to capture the birth, rushed into the room. I quickly read through their birth plan which was extensive, yet reasonable.

The photographer captured a perfect, beautiful, natural childbirth. Women pregnant with their first child often fantasize about having this type of delivery experience. (In reality, around 70–80% of laboring women get epidurals for their first delivery and after experiencing a bearable labor, most get epidurals on their subsequent deliveries as well.) Crystal and Brad's baby girl was born at 2:49 p.m.—less than 15 minutes after coming onto the unit. Crystal was on her hands and knees on the queen-size bed, quietly holding the headboard. She pushed through a handful of contractions while her midwife rubbed her back. I held a cool washcloth to her forehead, her doula offered sips of water and her husband, while supportive, stood back, wide-eyed, and let the women collectively do their thing.

Brad cried as their daughter took her first few breaths and quietly looked around. She was immediately placed skin to skin after Crystal rotated off her knees, onto her back. The infant was eagerly breastfeeding within minutes. This beautiful, dark-haired baby girl was named after Crystal's Buddhist mentor.

I had to take a rain check on my yoga class but I left work that day feeling more Zen than I usually do after a sweaty hour on my yoga mat. I had just been part of a spectacular birth; the kind pregnant women fantasize about while reading 'What to Expect When You're Expecting'.

I was giddy from the reality that I actually get paid to do this job.

Chapter 25
Praise Jesus

Martha was a beautiful woman. Her hair was coiffed and her nails were perfectly manicured. She was pregnant with her sixth baby—her first girl. Her eldest three sons were born naturally at full term, with no complications. Her next two sons were each born at 36 weeks. "I just went into labor early with both of the last two."

She came into OB Triage at 36 weeks with complaints of abdominal pain. She was in early labor and her baby's biophysical profile (BPP), collective information gathered through a bedside ultrasound, was only 4/10, indicating distress. The baby was also breech and the decision was made to do a primary C-section that same day.

Martha came to Labor & Delivery with Linda, her mother. Linda was very charismatic. She told me things like, "I am a prison warrior. I meet with rapers, robbers, murderers, and haters. I show them the Lord!" and "You so pretty with your gray hair!" and "Praise Jesus, it's the Lord's will she be born today!" and lots of, "Yes ma'am" this, "thank you ma'am" that.

Linda brought not one, but two phones into the operating room to take pictures and videos of the birth. "Praise Jesus, this is my first granddaughter!" When the baby was born, she was brought over to the warmer and handed off to the awaiting neonatal team. Linda, using both her loud voice and her elbows, demanded, "Can you move out the way of the video?"

As is very common with 36-week infants, the baby had secretions suctioned out of her mouth and stomach and she needed continuous positive airway pressure (CPAP) to help open up her lungs. When Linda saw what the neonatal nurses were doing, she became very upset. She shoved the neonatal nurse practitioner, grabbed at the mask and the suction tube and screamed, "You smothering my baby!" She threatened, "I'm gonna sue you all. Every last one of ya's. You killed my last grandbaby." Martha's sister had recently lost a baby at 22 weeks; Linda was emotionally triggered and clearly she thought she was fighting to save this grandbaby's life.

Security was called. They came to the operating room doors, saw the escalation, and quickly called the local police department. Linda was standing on her chair, hysterical. I repeatedly reassured Linda that we were all helping her baby and eventually she allowed only me to touch and resuscitate her granddaughter. The neonatal team stood helplessly off to the side. When Linda decided and stated "enough is enough", she shoved me away and again grabbed at the equipment.

The security team and the local police department wanted to physically remove Linda from the operating room but we were all afraid for the infant's safety and that of

Martha, who was undergoing major abdominal surgery. In the end, the physical presence of the security guard, standing in the corner of the operating room, was enough to compel Linda to settle down.

When we all left the operating room and headed to the recovery room, Linda was met at the door by one security guard and two police officers. They ushered her to a separate room and she visibly yielded to the authority figures. She was given an ultimatum: If you continue to behave like this and disrupt care for your daughter and/or your granddaughter, you will be physically escorted from the hospital and not allowed to return. She complied and then said to me, "I'm sorry for my behavior but I've had four people die in this hospital and you were killing my grandbaby!"

While in the recovery room, their pastor paid a visit. He was 6'4" and built like a bouncer. He came in wearing sunglasses, a bright neon green shirt and black slacks. He praised Jesus and prayed with Martha and Linda. When he was ready to leave, he placed his large hand on Linda's head. She sheepishly looked up at him and said, "Pastor, I don't think I can make it to church tonight. I'm so tired!"

He patted her head and said, "That's ok, Linda. You are excused for tonight."

This felt like it was the longest C-section I had ever been part of, which of course, is not true. There were so many unspoken, deep-seated systemic racism and gender issues at play. The OR staff were all white women (surgeon, resident, scrub tech, two nurses), the neonatal team were all white women (neonatal nurse practitioner, neonatal resident and nurse). The hospital security guards and the police officers were white men. Martha and Linda were Black.

The centuries-old systemic racism, health disparities, and prejudices materialized with the simple act of resuscitation—which to Linda, appeared aggressive, ridiculous and unnecessary. Martha remained quiet throughout the cesarean and Linda never stopped yelling, shoving, and fighting to protect her precious granddaughter. I do not believe she had any malicious intent. Fight or flight? She fought! I loved her for that.

Chapter 26
While Pleading for Help

It was the first Sunday in January, a frigid snowy start to the New Year. Yolanda, 21 years old, was on her way to have lunch with her family. 36 weeks pregnant with her third son, she was excited to spend time with her parents, her siblings and her nieces and nephews. Her two sons, ages three and five, were strapped in the backseat.

Unexpectedly and without warning, her small car stalled in the right-hand lane of the highway. Thankfully, she was able to guide the car over almost to the shoulder before it completely went dead: no flashers, steering or brakes. There was nowhere for Yolanda to escape the heavy, after-church traffic on a tricky, curvy section of the highway. On her left were three lanes of steady traffic and on her right, a cement embankment. She made a frantic phone call to her father and, while pleading for help, she likely never knew what hit her...

Around the curve behind her, driving too fast for the snowy conditions, came a Ford F-150 pickup truck driven by a man who never saw her car. He did not have time to even touch his brakes when he realized she was in his path.

Yolanda's father heard both her scream and the crash that crushed the back bumper of his daughter's car all the way to the dashboard. It took nearly two hours to extricate Yolanda and her two sons from the car before they could be sent to our nearby local hospital.

Yolanda was responsive and speaking in English when she arrived in the emergency room (ER) but it was difficult for the teams to understand her slurred words. Her unborn son was still alive, but distressed, with fetal heart tones in the 160's, the high side of normal. Her blood pressure was 160/100 (very high for a pregnant woman) and she was writhing in pain.

Several medical teams (ER, OR and OB) surrounded her stretcher, trying to decide how best to proceed with her care. Everyone was in agreement that she needed an emergency C-section while her baby was still alive, but they discovered through a STAT portable bedside x-ray that her pelvis was shattered and the skull of her unborn baby was also fractured.

When her condition abruptly went downhill, Yolanda transitioned to speaking Spanish (her native language) and it was very difficult for the interpreter to translate what she was saying. There was a collective "Oh shit" from the trauma bay staff fighting to save Yolanda's life. Without warning, her blood pressure dropped to 60/20 and Yolanda became unresponsive. Her baby still had a heartbeat. The team performed CPR and the decision was made to proceed immediately to the main operating room where an emergency cesarean section was performed to try to save Yolanda and her baby.

When the incision was made into her abdomen, the roughly 20 units (about 2.5 gallons) of blood that filled it poured out onto the floor. The surgeons discovered that she had suffered major trauma to the blood vessels that fed her liver and that was the source of most of her internal bleeding. She had already gone into disseminated intravascular coagulation (DIC), which means that her blood could no longer clot. She bled to death. Both Yolanda and her unborn son died on the operating room table.

Her 3-year-old son was taken to the intensive care unit where he was treated for multiple injuries and fractures, including his legs, spine and skull. He had internal bleeding, underwent multiple surgeries and died 10 days later. Miraculously, her 5-year-old son escaped with only minor facial lacerations.

The driver of the truck had not been drinking, nor was he on his phone. He survived without major injuries, but I can only imagine what he still carries.

Chapter 27
Influenza A

Jessica was a 22-year-old, married woman 30 weeks pregnant with her first baby. She was very healthy, without any significant medical or social history or perinatal risk factors.

On Saturday, a bitter cold New Year's Day, Jessica started to experience flu-like symptoms. Her husband took her to their local hospital emergency room where a flu swab was done, along with other bloodwork. All came back negative. She wasn't sure but she thought she'd had a flu shot that season, even though it couldn't be found anywhere in her records. She was sent home and encouraged to rest, drink plenty of fluids and follow up with her doctor on Monday if she wasn't feeling better.

Sunday, the following evening, she was still sick but acted "normal". She slept a lot but was able to eat dinner and was keeping liquids down. Monday morning, at 4:30 a.m., when she got up to use the bathroom, her husband reported that "She was fine, just a little weak."

Later Monday morning around 9:00 a.m., her husband was making breakfast when he heard a loud crash. He found

Jessica mostly unresponsive on the bathroom floor where she had fallen. She responded only to pain and was not able to answer any questions. He immediately called 9–1–1 and she was rushed to our hospital in an ambulance.

When she arrived in the emergency room, her fever was 103.2 degrees and her complete blood count showed that she was indeed fighting an infection of some sort. Influenza swabs and several other blood tests were sent to the lab. She was still mostly unresponsive. The bedside fetal monitor showed that her baby was alive. Then, Jessica had a grand mal seizure.

Interventional Radiology (IR) did a lumbar puncture which showed that she had influenza encephalitis infectious disease, caused by Influenza A. It was unclear at this point if the seizure had been brought on by the encephalitis or if Jessica had developed eclampsia. Her baby was still alive.

She was then sent to radiology for an MRI of her brain, which showed that she had acute disseminated encephalomyelitis (ADEM). This condition can develop following a viral or bacterial infection and can cause inflammation in the brain and spinal cord.

Jessica was admitted to the medical intensive care unit (MICU), fully sedated and placed on a ventilator. Her pupils were sluggish. Her baby was still alive.

Four days after the first onset of her symptoms, an intracranial pressure (ICP) monitor was placed to assess the pressure in her brain. Not surprisingly, her ICP was very high and there was concern of brain damage.

One week into the New Year, an electroencephalogram (EEG) was performed to evaluate her brain's electrical activity. Jessica's EEG showed a flatline, which meant that her brain was no longer alive. But her baby was. She remained in the ICU on full life support while her unborn baby was monitored and a plan for delivery was put into place.

The baby's heart rate was monitored continuously throughout Jessica's time in the ICU and had been running in the 150s. Less than 24 hours after the flatline EEG, Jessica spiked another high fever at which point her baby's heart rate became tachycardic (extremely fast), running in the 180s with shallow, spontaneous decelerations. Nine days into the New Year, Jessica went into labor and the baby began having late decelerations, indicating serious fetal distress. He was no longer tolerating being in-utero and needed to be delivered.

The decision was made to do a C-section. Despite her brain death, Propofol and Fentanyl were used, to be certain of her comfort during the surgery. No other anesthetic was used or needed. She had a major postpartum hemorrhage following the delivery and was treated for that with several different medications. Their son was born weighing 3½ pounds. With Apgar scores of 1 and 7, he went immediately to NICU and did quite well, despite his gestational age and circumstances surrounding his birth.

Prior to her C-section, the OB and ICU teams, along with Jessica's husband, Ryan, agreed that if necessary, she would be fully resuscitated in the operating room for the sake of the baby. Ryan agreed to the heartbreaking, recommended plan of care that would change Jessica's status to DNR (do not resuscitate) once the C-section was finished. A few hours after the birth of their son, the decision was made to start the Brain Death Protocol. Jessica was the talk of our unit for those nine long days—everyone hoping and praying that she'd take a turn for the better and survive.

Jessica died that night.

Maternal death is rare, something we (thankfully) don't experience very often. Both of these tragedies gripped the entire staff on Labor & Delivery: one trauma, the other illness—whether we were directly involved in providing care to these patients, or supporting and consoling our colleagues who were.

Chapter 28
The Day Before Thanksgiving

It was a typical Wednesday on the unit and I was working with a brand-new nurse who I was orienting to Labor & Delivery. I had plans to introduce her to the operating room, but the first scheduled C-section of the day wasn't until 11:30 a.m. which meant that she and I were "free" until 9:30 a.m. when our patient was expected to arrive. During our time together, I intended to take my orientee through the process of prepping our patient for surgery and orienting her to both the operating room and the recovery room. I also wanted to begin to teach her how important it is to bring a *why* into everything we do. Knowing *why* we do things is equally as important as knowing *what* to do. It was our first time working together.

At 7:00 a.m. the Labor & Delivery night-shift charge nurse was notified that a patient had just arrived in the emergency room (ER) having delivered her third baby in the car on the way to the hospital. She was bleeding heavily, suffering from a postpartum hemorrhage. We knew nothing else about the patient or her baby.

Another nurse from the unit, my orientee and I grabbed hemorrhage meds, a few other basic but important supplies and headed to the ER. We were not at all prepared for the chaos we walked into. The room was packed with nurses, residents and technicians, each busy with their respective jobs in this emergent situation. In addition, a full neonatal team surrounded the Panda Warmer (a special equipment bed used in Labor & Delivery with all newborn babies to warm them while pediatric assessments and interventions are done) and were urgently attending to the baby.

Tammy was moaning and writhing in pain on a stretcher that was soaked with blood and large blood clots. The attending obstetrician, appropriately concerned about the active bleeding, was quickly attempting to do a manual removal of clots and uterine contents. Placental fragments were removed, but her bleeding continued and there were most assuredly more pieces of her placenta remaining inside. (These placental fragments can cause infection and more bleeding.) Tammy also had a second-degree perineal laceration (tear) that would need to be repaired. A second IV was started, hemorrhage medications were administered and she was given morphine to help relieve her pain.

Randall, Tammy's husband, arrived in the room after parking their car, sweating and clearly distressed. He was visibly torn between his wife and his newborn daughter. What made matters worse was that Randall suffered from significant hearing loss. He could only understand words that he could read off the lips of the person speaking to him. He had to be looked at directly and spoken to slowly.

Unfortunately, this case happened during the Covid pandemic and everyone in the room was wearing a mask.

There was nothing slow or quiet going on in that room. There was no one with an unassigned task who could give Randall the kind of deliberate, unmasked and enunciated speech he needed and deserved.

At about the same time that the team was trying to update Randall, the neonatologist told Tammy that the baby, a girl they had named Hanna, was being transported to the neonatal intensive care unit (NICU) for the care that was necessary. Hanna was nearly full term at 38 weeks gestation, but she had multiple anomalies: spina bifida (a condition where the spine and spinal cord don't form properly), an omphalocele (a birth defect of the abdominal wall), multiple heart defects and Trisomy 13 (a rare and lethal genetic disorder). Tammy looked intently at the neonatologist and calmly said, despite her obvious physical discomfort, "She's not going anywhere. She's gonna die and she's staying with me."

We later learned that Tammy and Randall had received extensive counseling during the pregnancy and knew that Hanna's anomalies were lethal. They knew that she would not live outside the uterus for very long. They had made arrangements for their pastor to bless her, a photographer to capture her short life with pictures, and palliative care to keep her as comfortable as possible. They had written several songs to sing to her and their other children, ages three and five.

Tammy and Hanna were transferred to Labor & Delivery together, skin to skin. Hanna appeared pink and stable. Tammy continued to bleed and pass clots but was also stable. Because she had previously had a C-section, the doctors were concerned that the remaining placental fragments might be embedded in her uterine scar. This would require emergency surgery. The neonatologist came to see Hanna and talked with Tammy and Randall about their plans and how to best keep her comfortable: skin to skin, breastfeed if Hanna showed interest or ability (acknowledging that this was unlikely), no shots or IV, unless deemed necessary for her comfort.

Tammy and Randall were in full agreement.

At 8:00 a.m., I did an assessment and found Hanna's heart rate to be in the 150s, her respiratory rate in the 40s and non-labored, her color pink. These were all normal findings and overall, she was doing as well as could be expected. The hope was that she would survive until the rest of the extended family arrived from out of town to meet her. They were expected to arrive by 9:30 a.m.

While we were caring for Hanna, Tammy was given additional morphine. Her perineal laceration was repaired with a local anesthetic and one final attempt was made to manually remove the retained placenta, by scraping the inside of the uterus with a specialized instrument called a banjo curette. The removal attempt was painful and unsuccessful. Tammy continued to bleed heavier than normal. Having already lost over 1.5 liters of blood, the decision was made to take Tammy to the main operating room for a dilation and curettage (D&C) under general anesthesia to remove the remaining placental fragments.

While Tammy was being attended to, Randall was doing skin to skin with Hanna. Their two other children (who had arrived with their grandmother) were both at his side melting down. The 5-year-old needed to "go potty" but refused to go without her mother. The 3-year-old whined,

"I hungry" as tears ran down his cheeks. They were both scared and wanted only their mother.

At 8:25 a.m. Randall said, in a panic, "Hanna is blue and gasping." I took her from him and gently laid her in the Panda Warmer. Her heart rate was now 75 and she was dusky and blue, breathing irregularly. I realized that Hanna was probably dying. At that exact moment, the charge nurse came into the room and said that the surgical team was on their way to get Tammy for her D&C.

I quickly tucked Hanna skin to skin with Tammy and wrapped them both in a warm blanket. When the attending OB came into the room, I explained the situation and asked if perhaps we could wait 10–15 minutes so that Tammy was not taken away from her dying daughter. Her bleeding was stable enough so she was given another 15 minutes with Hanna. By 8:45 a.m., not all that surprisingly, skin to skin proved itself once again to be the best intervention. By the end of her extra 15 minutes with Tammy, Hanna was pink, her heart rate back in the 150s and her respiratory efforts appeared unlabored and normal.

At 9:00 a.m., Tammy was taken to surgery and Hanna was placed skin to skin with Randall. The kids each had a snack and a phone to play with. The photographer was taking a multitude of pictures and the pastor sat quietly next to Randall.

Tammy's D&C took care of her bleeding and she was stable when she was brought back to the room. Hanna lived until late that afternoon, when she died peacefully in her parents' loving arms while they sang lullabies they had written for her.

It was the day before Thanksgiving. One could think that in a situation like this there isn't much to be thankful for, but Tammy and Randall talked specifically about their gratitude—that they knew going into the delivery what to expect and that they had the opportunity to plan and make arrangements ahead of time, allowing them to be present with Hanna in the most meaningful way for as long as possible.

I was thankful for the opportunity to care for them and witness their courageous love and focused intention, to learn from them, to grieve and celebrate with them. We smiled and cried; they took pictures, prayed and sang softly to Hanna.

I was grateful for the opportunity to walk through this shift with my orientee, introducing her to an entirely unexpected type of patient care, hopeful that our time together would help shape her into the compassionate nurse she was meant to become. Early in my career, my preceptor explained to me that patients often arrive feeling both scared and anxious, and that sharing in that fear, especially during a crisis, doesn't help. Patients can sense your anxiety and/or your calmness, which either serves to intensity or regulate their own, complicating or improving their treatment and outcome.

Chapter 29
Never Judge a Book

On a steamy Wednesday morning in August, I met Maria, a 28-year-old woman scheduled for her seventh C-section. The night-shift nurse had gotten her ready for surgery and gave me a very thorough report about Maria's medical and psycho/social history. The information made me a bit nervous. It was likely that at least some of the issues, laid out before me like candy in a dish, would show up in the operating room. Maria's history included six prior cesareans, anxiety, depression and domestic abuse. She had no history of alcohol, tobacco or substance use. Her children were fathered by three different men. She had her first baby at age 16.

Her first two children, both boys, were with a physically abusive man whose name was never mentioned. Thankfully, she had managed to extricate herself and end the relationship with him. He is no longer involved with her or their children.

Her next two sons were fathered by a man who was incarcerated. Maria temporarily lost custody of these first 4 children after her 9-year-old son shot his 7-year-old brother with a gun found in her home and child protective services (CPS) got involved. Thankfully, the gunshot wound did not cause serious injury.

The father of her current baby, as well as her last two children, was a drug dealer who had recently been shot multiple times during a drug deal gone wrong. After his hospitalization and rehab, he went to prison. Maria's parents had custody of the two youngest boys.

This baby was a girl who was to be named Siete Amor. Lucky #7. When I actually met Maria, I saw a beautiful woman who stood less than 5 feet tall. Her hair had long, dark pink braids and her nails were painted a soft, pale pink. She had braces on her teeth and multiple tattoos covering her body. On the front of her right thigh was a scripture passage from Isaiah. Laughing and simultaneously rolling her eyes when I tried to read the tattoo, her grandmother said, "*Her body looks like a newspaper!*"

Maria told me she always wanted ten kids but decided to have her tubes tied during this cesarean because, "I finally got my girl!"

Her mother and grandmother were her support system. They had both left Cuba for the Dominican Republic and had ultimately landed in the United States. They were bilingual, friendly, talkative everyday women. Interestingly enough, they were also both licensed pilots.

They talked about how much they loved family time, reading the Bible and finding creative ways to use passion fruit. (Parcha Juice being their "absolute favorite!" They put it in ice cube trays to make "smoothies for the adults and slushies for the kids"). They were beautiful, ordinary, respectful people.

The surgery was uneventful. Maria was breastfeeding Siete Amor before we even left the operating room, which she said she planned to do for a year. "Breastfeeding is the best thing we can do for our babies," she said with a sincere smile on her face.

I had the pleasure of meeting four generations of connected women. Strong, resilient, smart women. Based on the report I received at the start of my shift, this was not what I expected to see or be part of. It was a consummate reminder of how important it is to withhold judgment of a patient before you meet them. Never judge a book by its cover, so they say.

When I kept my mind and heart open, my patients were never one-dimensional like our biases can make them. In fact, the delivery room is a vulnerable space where humanity unfolds, powerful emotions surface, and relationship dynamics are punctuated. I bore witness to this that day.

Chapter 30
Abundant Faith

Laura and Thomas were a married, conservative Christian couple with 9 children at home—a mix of biological (6) and adopted (4). All of their children were girls, with the exception of one adopted boy, who died from a congenital heart defect during the adoption process. Life was centered around their faith and their children. They spoke softly but firmly that God was in charge. "It is up to God to decide how many children we have, not us. Each child is truly a gift from God." Although it hadn't always been possible, they believed in having natural, unmedicated childbirth deliveries.

When I met them, Laura was 38 years old and 32 weeks pregnant with her seventh biological daughter. Sadly, although Laura had not had enough of being pregnant, her uterus had. At her routine 20-week ultrasound, they were devastated to learn that Laura had placenta previa with possible placenta accreta—her placenta was covering her cervix and there was an area that looked like the placenta was deeply attached to the wall of her uterus (by way of the uterine incision scar from a prior C-section). Not only did

Laura struggle to accept the fact that this would be her last baby, but also that because she would have to go under general anesthesia for the surgery, she and Thomas would both miss the birth of their last daughter altogether.

Due to the high risk of intraoperative hemorrhage, placenta accreta is considered a potentially life-threatening condition with an estimated 7–9% maternal mortality rate. In cases like this, a cesarean hysterectomy (removing the uterus without delivering the placenta) is needed, under general anesthesia, in order to reduce the risk of blood loss and hemorrhage. A prearranged, detailed, multidisciplinary surgical plan for this specialized procedure—often involving 15–20 different staff members—is critical for survival of both mother and infant. Because this is such a high-risk, complicated surgery, it is scheduled in the main operating room instead of the Labor & Delivery operating room.

I began Laura's initial surgical prep in Labor & Delivery (fetal monitor strip, IV start, full medical and pregnancy history). She then met individually with each surgeon and multidisciplinary team member before being transferred to the main operating room. While the environment in Labor & Delivery is normally calm and quiet, the main operating room gets loud and bustling when all of the teams merge together into that one big room. For Laura's surgery, those teams included:

- **Maternal Fetal Medicine:** performing the cesarean section (delivery of the baby) and coordinating the care.

- **Gynecology Oncology**: performing the hysterectomy.
- **Urology**: placing ureteral stents to easily identify and protect her ureters, which carry urine from her kidneys to her bladder.
- **Anesthesiology**: placing an arterial line to more closely monitor her vital signs and administering general anesthesia, medications and blood products as needed.
- **Obstetrics Nursing and Surgical Nursing Teams**: responsibility for baby and baby equipment, patient prep, managing specialized equipment and surgical supplies, communication across teams and documentation of each phase during the surgery.
- **Specialized Technicians (Perfusionists)**: operating the Cell Saver machine for autologous transfusion—safely collecting, separating and returning Shannon's own red blood cells back to her. Multiple units of stored packed red blood cells, platelets and fresh frozen plasma, all cross matched and double-checked, were also on hand in the operating room for Laura (if needed).
- **Neonatology**: receiving the premature, anesthetized baby (Laura had been under general anesthesia for over 60 minutes before the baby was born) and transferring her from the operating room to the NICU.

Once Laura was transferred to the main operating room, there was a group huddle with all team members present.

The lead surgeon, the gynecologic oncologist, listened to the plan and the order in which the events would take place, as presented by each member of the team. This group huddle takes time. It promotes patient safety by helping to ward off any unexpected problems or complications once the surgery is underway. The huddle reminds me of the moving, powerful prayer circles that happen in church; we gather together, make eye contact and use soft voice tones to communicate our words and needs, all with a sense of camaraderie, strength and positive energy, with only one person speaking at a time.

Laura's surgery took four hours. The OB and neonatal teams left the main operating room after the baby was delivered, stabilized and transferred to the NICU. (The remaining steps of the surgery were completed by the main OR teams.) Later that afternoon, when I saw her anesthesiologist, he told me that everything had gone smoothly and according to plan—no hemorrhage and no need for a blood transfusion. Laura remained very stable and was transferred to a regular postpartum floor for her recovery. Her daughter was also doing very well in the NICU.

Laura was discharged from the hospital four days later. Countless prayers had been answered.

When I took care of Laura and Thomas, I was acutely aware of their shared common pathway. For them, it was their strong Christian faith that gave them solidarity, a strength that allowed them to be so present with each other, so connected. I felt honored to be drawn in and welcomed by this dynamic duo. They were calm, settled, patient, and quiet. Intensely committed to listening to each other first, which, in turn, ultimately helped them to be able to hear what each of the different teams had to say. This can be an emotionally charged few hours prior to surgery in the best cases, and patients without some sort of pathway to help them self-regulate, often don't manage themselves this well.

Chapter 31
They Have No Voice

Expected to Remain Silent

Hiba was from Sudan and she spoke no English. Her husband Salim spoke for her. With his broken English, he answered every question directed toward her. With a consensual nod to Salim, she refused interpretation services—rendering herself virtually voiceless, with no say in her care. It appeared as though she was expected to remain speechless throughout the entire duration of her labor and delivery. She was expected to endure the pain of labor silently.

Hiba's face expressed no emotions, yet in her eyes, I saw deep agony. Her silence is where I heard her loudest truths. Hiba had no mother or sisters with her, no sign of her other children. Just Salim and what appeared to be her conspicuous resignation to the life that was handed to her. Her withdrawal and detachment were as chilling as the sight of her genitals.

Hiba was a victim of female genital mutilation (FGM). All of her clitoris, as well as most of her labia minora and/or majora had been removed. The associated scar tissue was prominent and added searing agony to her already painful, unmedicated delivery.

Hiba was a vessel to silently bear children. Repeatedly. I was witness to babies number 9 and 11.

According to the World Health Organization (WHO), FGM has happened to more than 200 million girls and women who are alive today in 30 countries in Africa, the Middle East and Asia. FGM typically occurs between infancy and 15 years of age. Treatment of health complications from FGM costs the US health systems $1.4 billion/year. FGM is recognized internationally as a violation of the human rights of girls and women. It reflects deep-rooted inequality between the sexes and constitutes an extreme form of discrimination against girls.

This was an exceptionally difficult case for me. I struggled mightily to set aside my own cultural and gender biases. There appeared to be no other gender role-playing options for either Hiba or Salim. He had likely been raised to be in control of her and she was taught that she had no voice, it had been mutilated by the patriarchy. He appeared attentive, comfortable with this command and yet he showed no empathy for her labor pain or discomfort. Hiba was detached, miserable and mute.

I will never understand or accept female genital mutilation. I know that I will never not see it as both physically and emotionally damaging to my sex—to my fellow women, to all women. I know that the enemy of violence and harm toward others, particularly those we love, is empathy. I wonder how he lost empathy for his wife, how he lost the connection to his heart and became a vessel in the cruelty of extreme patriarchy.

"If You Didn't Eat So Much Ice Cream"

Marisol came into my care when she arrived to have her labor induced with her third baby. She told me the reason for her induction was that she was struggling to keep her diabetes under control—"For some reason, this third pregnancy has just been so hard."

Her husband, William ("but please, call me Bill"), once he was assured that I knew he was an orthodontist in town, rolled his eyes and said, "Well, if you didn't eat so much ice cream before bed every night, it probably would NOT have been so difficult." Marisol blushed, softly chuckled, nodded her head and looked to the floor.

When I was reviewing Marisol's health history and plan of care, we started to discuss pain control options for her once she got into labor. Bill, who had become increasingly more agitated the more I spoke, interrupted me and said, "Marisol won't be using any pain medicine and she for sure isn't having a needle stuck in her back for an epidural!" Again, Marisol was silent and her gaze went to the floor, perhaps from embarrassment, or to lessen the loneliness she felt making eye contact with Bill. Or perhaps it was the pain she'd feel from seeing my look of concern for her.

I had not asked for his opinion about her pain management options. So many domestic violence (DV) red flags were flying that I had to resist the urge to let words of alarm and assertive patient advocacy fly out of my mouth.

I needed to proceed cautiously in asking Marisol if she felt safe with Bill, inquiring without judgement whether he had hurt her physically, verbally, or emotionally. It wasn't until the very end of my shift that I could finally get Marisol alone. Bill had taken an emergency phone call from his office and because he was preoccupied on the couch, he waved his hand, flippantly giving his consent that I could help Marisol to the bathroom. (He had accompanied her *every* other time.)

When she sat down on the toilet, she looked embarrassed and defeated, yet relieved that I was with her. I asked her, "Marisol, are you ok?" Tears were in her eyes, her lip quivered, and she looked at the floor, subtly shaking her head side to side. I chose to be more succinct, more direct with my concern, knowing that our time alone was limited. I kneeled on the floor so that our eyes were level, I touched her shoulder and gently said, "Marisol, can you please look at me?" She slowly raised her eyes and her tears started to flow. I said, "Is your relationship with Bill safe? Has he ever hurt you?"

She shook her head some more, looked back at the floor and weakly said, "No, it's fine. Everything's fine."

In my gut, I knew that what I suspected (DV) was true and she knew that I knew. I quietly spoke these words to her, "I realize how difficult this is to talk about. I am here to help you. We are all here to help you. You can talk to any of us at any time and we will help make a safety plan for you and all of your children."

Bill knocked loudly on the door and questioned, as if to start an interrogation, "What's going on in there? What's taking so long?" His voice sounded edgy, angry. I stepped out of the bathroom and nonchalantly shut the door behind me to give Marisol time to collect herself. I saw no empathy or concern in his eyes. I started to feel afraid.

I said to him, "Marisol is getting uncomfortable with her labor so it is taking her a bit longer than usual. She has finished using the bathroom and is going to brush her teeth and wash her hands and face real quick, she'll be right out." He scowled at me, clearly deciding whether or not to go into the bathroom. I stood my ground and spontaneously thought to offer him a cup of coffee as a distraction. He refused the offer, went back to the couch and picked up his phone.

For Marisol's sake, I certainly did not want to incite Bill's anger. I was both thankful that the distraction worked and also that he refused the coffee. That meant I didn't have to leave the room to go get it and I would be present when Marisol emerged from the bathroom. I went to the computer and started charting, waiting for Marisol to come back to bed.

The nurse who would be taking over Marisol's care came into the room just as Marisol opened the bathroom door. Marisol's face was washed, she had applied lip gloss and there was no sign of her tears. She asked if she could sit in the rocking chair next to the fetal monitor. (This was notably the furthest that she could be away from Bill in the labor room.) The new nurse and I simultaneously made sure she was comfortable in her new rocking chair position as I gave the next nurse the bedside report. I said goodbye to Marisol and Bill and wished them all the best with their new baby.

Once I left the room, I sent a text to Marisol's new nurse and asked her to come to the desk when she could. No hurry.

I would wait. I needed to tell her my concerns, the dynamics that I had witnessed and Marisol's response to my bathroom inquiry. I could not safely share this information at the bedside for Marisol's sake. I encouraged the next nurse to screen Marisol again and to watch over her very closely.

Both of these cases came home with me. I wondered if I could or should have done something differently, said something better. Did they know how much I cared about them and their safety? I was scared for them both. I worried about Hiba's wretched despondency and Marisol's physical and emotional well-being. And their combined 14 children.

Domestic violence (DV) knows no boundary. The rigid gender scripts—verbosity vs. silence, control vs. powerlessness—sadly reared its ugliness, at times, in the delivery room no matter the class or ethnicity. We know that pregnancy is one of the greatest risk factors for escalation of violence. The perpetrator can feel as if he is second string to the baby and to his wife, who gets all the attention during the pregnancy, labor and the delivery. When, for most fathers, this is a time to open their hearts to an addition to their growing family, instead, these broken and insecure partners are threatened.

As a labor nurse, I was responsible for screening every patient, every visit, for their safety at home. (When I first started in Labor & Delivery, domestic violence was not talked about unless a woman came in with bruises after being assaulted.) I was expected to ask difficult questions about the safety of my patient's intimate relationship. I also learned that asking questions about domestic violence is something that should NEVER be done in front of any partner. Simply asking the questions can bring on brutality. "Why'd she ask you that?"/"What did you tell her?"/"What made her think that something is wrong with us or with you?"

Sometimes it was difficult to get my patient alone, separate from her domineering partner, to do the screening in private. I often found the only way I could get the patient alone was when I would make an excuse to follow her into the bathroom and shut the door (i.e., "let me show you how to measure your urine", "here are pads and panties", "here are the supplies for you to take a shower, brush your teeth", etc.).

The more abusive and controlling a partner is, the more likely they are to not leave the patient's side, especially when caregivers are in the room. They accompany the patient to the bathroom. They bring all their food from home so they don't have to go to the cafeteria. They often act entitled to use the patient's bathroom, without asking permission, instead of the public restroom. This makes it very difficult to screen these patients for domestic violence.

We know that it can take asking a victim of domestic violence an average of 8–10 times before they will admit to the abuse, that they are in an unsafe relationship/situation and to acknowledge that they and their children need help. The labor room should never be a place where an expectant mother needs to worry that her partner could hijack her emotional and physical safety with his insecurity. Persistence is key to helping the victim begin to escape the abuse.

Female genital mutilation happens to female children and pre-adolescents who are underage, with no rights of their own. Intimate partner violence (IPV), the term used to discuss violence between intimate partners, is mostly between adults, both men and women.

Domestic violence, intimate partner violence, and female genital mutilation all inflict severe harm on both the body and the voice of women through oppression. Control is exerted by the perpetrator, whether in cultures that condone male dominance, such as those where genital mutilation is practiced, or in the United States, where alarming rates of abuse occur.

Chapter 32
Babymoon

Kathryn and Trevor were high-school sweethearts who started dating when they were 16 years old. They were both physically fit, active and popular. The perfect match. They married right after college and started their careers in Chicago. When they decided to start a family, they moved back to their hometown with their dog and bought a house close to their families.

When she was 15 years old, Kathryn was diagnosed with Type 1 diabetes. She never complained about it and managed her blood sugar with an insulin pump, a strict diet and regular exercise. The ideal patient.

Kathryn was 29 years old and 31 weeks pregnant with their first baby. The pregnancy had been uneventful, so she and Trevor decided to fly to Florida for a long weekend "babymoon". It was March, the perfect time of year to travel south in search of sunshine, fresh air and time together before the baby makes three.

After a lovely weekend away, they flew home on Sunday afternoon, in time to prepare for the work week ahead. After dinner, Kathryn changed her insulin pump, per her usual routine. They showered and went to bed around 9:00 p.m. Trevor went right to sleep but Kathryn laid awake. Her stomach didn't feel right. She thought it might be a little constipation. After using the bathroom and feeling a little relief, she went back to bed.

But she couldn't get comfortable. She tossed and turned, trying to figure out why she was having so much pain in her hips. When the pain moved into her back and her legs, her Apple watch alerted her that her blood sugar was in the 300 range. This was very unusual for her, especially in the middle of the night. *Must be a new pump site issue*, she thought. *Or maybe I just had one too many virgin pina coladas in Florida.* She stayed in bed until the pain was so intense that it made her sick. After she ran to the bathroom and vomited, she woke Trevor up and they called her doctor.

Kathryn didn't give the doctor much information about her blood sugar or the pain. She assumed all of her symptoms were related to having been on vacation and feeling constipated. The doctor suggested that she treat the symptoms of constipation in the morning and come into the office for evaluation if she wanted to. The doctor also told her to pay attention to how much the baby was moving.

She laid back down and tried to sleep, but the pain kept getting worse. Her blood sugar continued to run in the 300 range, despite giving herself extra insulin and still having had nothing to eat. This was a big red flag for Kathryn. She also realized that she hadn't felt the baby move much at all since earlier in the night. Kathryn was not a complainer, so Trevor knew by how she was acting that there was cause for concern. They decided it was time to go to the hospital.

They took nothing with them as they were certain they would be sent home.

Arriving at the hospital at 6:15 a.m., Kathryn was put in an OB Triage room and quickly placed on the fetal monitor. She was feeling constant pain in her left lower abdomen and hips, but felt no pain in her belly where she thought contractions would hurt. She didn't think she was in labor. According to the monitor, however, she was having contractions, one right after the other, with no break in-between. Even though she did not have any vaginal bleeding, her abdomen was rigid, indicating a possible placental abruption. The placenta is the infant's lifeline—ensuring blood flow and oxygen. A placental abruption (when the placenta separates from the uterine wall before delivery) can be catastrophic to the baby.

Unborn babies speak to us with their heartbeats. The heart rate for Kathryn and Tyler's baby showed a Category III tracing—no (absent) variability, meaning it looked as though someone had used a sharp pencil to draw a straight line on the monitor paper. The baby was also having repetitive late decelerations, her heart rate dipping down after each contraction. All of this indicated that the placenta wasn't working sufficiently and that the baby was in severe fetal distress. Delivery needed to happen immediately. An IV was started, blood was drawn and quickly sent to the lab, and they were transferred upstairs to a delivery room.

I had gotten to work early that morning and was sitting at the main desk, checking my email. The charge nurse was sitting next to me when she received a phone call from OB Triage letting her know that "a 31-weeker is abrupting and she's coming up right now." Shit. It was 6:40 in the morning, just before shift change. It had been a very busy night on the unit and change of shift emergencies can be very difficult to manage.

I was not clocked in yet and didn't know any details, but as Kathryn rolled around the corner into a labor room, I asked the charge nurse if she wanted my help. After hearing "YES PLEASE!", I threw on a surgical cap and mask and went to the labor room where a STAT C-section was being called by the attending physician. I jumped in.

I introduced myself to Kathryn and made deliberate eye contact with her despite the chaos. I told her that I would be with her the whole time and that I'd see her when she woke up.

We were planning general anesthesia so Trevor could not come with us to the operating room. He was left all alone in the labor room. Remarkably calm as we said goodbye, tears were streaming down his cheeks, soaking his mask, required due to the Covid-19 pandemic.

When we rolled into the operating room one minute later, all I knew was that we had a 31-week baby who was in serious trouble and fighting for her life. I knew that Kathryn was a Type 1 diabetic with blood sugars out of control. I knew that she had no allergies to any medications and that she was having her first baby, a girl (one of the random questions someone asked her.) She was calm, compliant, and very scared. She tolerated the commotion of the team preparing for emergency surgery and did exactly as she was instructed, all while answering the barrage of last-minute important questions before she was put under general anesthesia.

The C-section was quickly underway with the neonatal team present and ready. During our quick handoff, the triage nurse showed me the baby's fetal heart rate tracing. I had known that we were in an emergency situation, but it wasn't until seeing that ominous monitor strip that I became very concerned. I did not know if this baby girl would be born alive or not.

At 6:52 a.m.—just 12 minutes after getting the call from OB Triage—Kathryn and Trevor's daughter Olive was born. She had poor Apgar scores. She was born with a very low heart rate, she was limp and cyanotic (blue), not breathing on her own, or moving any of her extremities. She required full resuscitation and was quickly transferred to the neonatal intensive care unit (NICU) on a ventilator. The blood gases in her umbilical cord were 6.9 In Labor & Delivery we know that 6.9 is just in time and 6.8 is too late. Olive had arrived just in time.

When examining the placenta in the operating room, the doctor did in fact see evidence of a placental abruption. Our earlier conclusion was correct.

Kathryn and Trevor's connection was one that I will never forget. In the midst of all the unexpected chaos inherent in a crisis such as this, what struck me then and has stayed with me since, was their eye contact, their tender and gentle touch. The way that they talked with each other spoke volumes about their love. We often dismiss high-school sweethearts as temporary, immature and not capable of a powerful, long-term connection. Kathryn and Trevor show us differently.

When I was pulled into crisis situations in my job, I rushed in and out of my patients' lives at such a pivotal moment, busy with tasks at hand, that I often didn't have enough time with them nor did I give myself permission to take in everything that I witnessed. This delivery was powerful, different for me. I took it all in. Because of the extraordinary love and connection that I witnessed here, this birth gave me great hope for humanity.

Chapter 33
Throuple

I met Madison on the day she was scheduled to have her first baby, a baby boy. She was scheduled for a C-section because she had been diagnosed with suspected macrosomia and polyhydramnios during her pregnancy—meaning that she was carrying a large baby and lots of extra amniotic fluid. A vaginal delivery with a baby this size was unlikely and potentially unsafe.

When I walked into her room to meet her and start her IV, I was surprised to see that there were two men at her bedside. I introduced myself and asked the question I ask every patient, "Who do you have here with you today?"

Pointing to a heavyset, bearded, bald man on the left, she said, "Oh, this is my husband, Gavin." Pointing to the thin, curly-haired, much younger man on the right, she said, "And this is my boyfriend, Brody."

Her direct, nonchalant response caught me off-guard. It's not every day you have a husband and a boyfriend present for a delivery. "Nice to meet you both," I said, warmly greeting them both. While getting Madison ready for surgery, I asked her which partner would be going back to the operating room with us.

Her husband raised his hand and said, "It'll be me."

The surgery went smoothly, without any complications. Her son, Elliott, was a beautiful, poster-child baby. He had a head full of curly brown hair and eyelashes that could be seen from six feet away.

I asked Gavin if he wanted to hold the baby. "Yes please," was his nervous response.

It was evident from the beginning that he wanted to love and bond with this baby. He spoke to him softly and gently cradled him, while at the same time, I imagine that he was wondering if this was his biological son or not. Earlier in our conversation, they shared that paternity was unknown and that they would do testing later to determine the biological father.

When the surgery was done, we went to the recovery room where Brody was anxiously awaiting our return. When Madison and Brody made eye contact, they both started crying. There was no question about which two were married and which two were in love.

Both men stayed at Madison's side throughout her time in recovery, assisting her with breastfeeding and feeding her ice chips. Both were sending pictures to friends and family members. They all lived together and were talking about how excited they were to take Elliott home and introduce him to their two dogs.

Although having both the husband and boyfriend in the same delivery room was initially disconcerting and unprecedented for me, their level of respect and civility toward each other was truly captivating. It led me to believe that Elliot was in good hands.

This delivery happened one week before I retired. Proof that I WILL NEVER SEE IT ALL!

Chapter 34
Tattoos: A Collective Chapter

As you can imagine, I have seen a lot of skin—and by association, a lot of ink. The body art ranged from beautiful and tasteful to repulsive, with everything in-between. These stories are mostly mine. Others come from my co-workers who filled my inbox with their recollections.

THERESE was a beautiful, fit woman who was in the operating room for her scheduled repeat C-section. She was being prepped for her spinal anesthesia when I heard the anesthesiologist say with a chuckle, "That's a nice tattoo."

I looked at her back and saw that he was referring to a very large "HELLO KITTY" tattoo, centered perfectly in the middle of her back.

Therese said, "Ya know, not once did my 18-year-old self-consider how embarrassed my 39-year-old self would be by that tattoo! I should've just gotten a bumper sticker for my car."

ISABELLE had been in labor for two days when the decision was made to do a C-section. While I was prepping her belly for surgery, the doctor was talking to her about the "bikini line" incision that would be made during surgery. She noticed that "Matthew" was tattooed exactly where the incision needed to go and said, "I would normally plan to put your incision right where that tattoo is but if you'd prefer, I could go a little above it. It's too low for me to go beneath it."

Isabelle laughed out loud and said, "Oh please, that was a drunk one-night stand. A really stupid idea. Please cut it out!" That's exactly what the surgeon did.

BETHANY was diagnosed with Stage 4 metastatic colorectal cancer during her third pregnancy. She suffered from tremendous pain, primarily in her rectum where she had a large golf-ball-sized tumor. She found it almost impossible to sit down so she rested on her side mostly, taking as many narcotics as we could give her for the pain.

I met her when it was time for her to be delivered at 34 weeks. Prior to her arrival on the unit, I had read through the plan of care written by her palliative care team. I was prepared to do my best for her, especially under such difficult circumstances. She knew she would not live to see her children grow up.

What I was not prepared for was her husband when he walked into her room. His face was covered in tattoos. His eyes were circled in black ink with eyelashes on top and bottom. He looked like the Raggedy Ann doll I had as a young child. Skeleton teeth circled his mouth in an oval shape, spreading onto his cheeks. He had a swastika tattooed on each side of his bald head, above his ears. His neck was tattooed a solid black up to his chin as if he were wearing a turtleneck sweater. On his right hand, 4 fingers said L-O-V-E. On his left, H-A-T-E.

He was gentle, kind and duly concerned about the premature birth of his son and his dying wife. Watching staff see him for the first time was disquieting. Some were visibly shocked, others were repulsed and, at times, speechless.

During my time with him, I found myself wanting to protect him from judgment and rejection based on his appearance. In my years as a Labor & Delivery nurse, I learned that physical appearances can be both telling and misleading, challenging me to remain open to the humanity that lies behind bodily ornaments of tattoos, clothing, makeup, and jewelry.

LAUREN refused to remove her t-shirt. I told her that if she were to need a C-section or an epidural, the shirt would have to come off. I also told her it would be much easier to remove the t-shirt before I started her IV. She still refused, saying she would only take it off if I could guarantee that her parents, who were coming for the delivery, wouldn't see it. They were very conservative and would "kill" her if they knew she had gotten a tattoo.

She finally consented when I told her we could try and keep her covered with a second gown worn backward. When she finally took her shirt off, I saw the tattoo that covered most of her chest, the top of her shoulders and her upper back. It was unobjectionable, but something her parents just wouldn't agree with. I couldn't imagine how she would ever keep that from her parents…no tank top or swimsuit for the rest of her life? At least we were successful keeping it a secret for the rest of my shift.

DANIELLE had a tattoo of lush greenery that covered her entire abdomen. When I complimented her on the tattoo, she laughed a little and thanked me. It wasn't until after her delivery in the operating room that I realized what I had complimented her on. One of the docs said, "We need to be careful with the staples to get the marijuana leaf back together straight. She probably spent a lot of time and money on this."

Other memorable designs:

- Inner thigh, from kneecap to groin—a brightly colored, dripping double-scoop ice cream cone which read "*Lick me til I drip*".

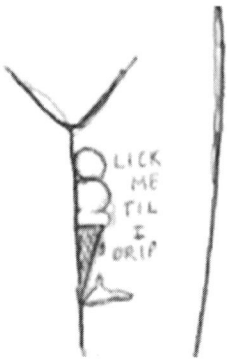

- Pubic bone to just beneath the breasts—a ring of jungle cats: lynx, lion, tiger, leopard, cheetah, and jaguar, entwined like monkeys in the game, *Barrel of Monkeys*.
- Upper pubic area:
  - "Property of Derrick" (Plot twist, Derrick was not the father of the baby.)
  - "Eat me" (It wasn't surprising that this patient was a cage fighter.)
  - "Kurt Bryant's House" with an arrow pointing down (The father of the baby was Charlie.)

- "Slippery when wet" cat eyes and ears (her pubic hair forming the nose of the cat).

- "Lick me" with a tongue.
- A patient was shaved from bottom to top—a Gila monster reptile in the strike position covered her pubic area. It literally gave me a scare.
- "Lick it or stick it".
- "Magically delicious" with Lucky Charm marshmallow shapes below.
• Inner thighs—pawprints going up the inside.

• Collarbone—a gorgeous daisy.

- Upper thigh—"Darker the cherry, sweeter the juice" with several cherries.

- Back of thighs—"Fuck me like a rockstar".
- Belly down to pubic bone—"Enter here" with an arrow pointing down. When she sat up for her epidural, I was surprised by the second arrow pointing down on her lower back that said, "or here".
- Front thigh—"Yes sir" with a side profile of a woman's face with two fingers in her mouth.
- Butt cheek:
  - "USDA PRIME" like a cattle stamp.

- "JUICY" in large, block calligraphy letters like Juicy Couture.
- "GRL PWR" ("Girl Power" and not surprisingly, she delivered unmedicated).

- Across the stomach, distorted by stretch marks: "TMNT" (Teenage Mutant Ninja Turtles).
- Inner thighs—"Expensive" with dollar signs.
- Areolas—hearts tattooed on both.
- Upper back—a seated, naked woman masturbating with legs wide open, surrounded in flames.

Father of the baby requested a copy of the baby's footprints for a tattoo on his forearm.

Father of the baby got a "due date" tattoo rather than a tattoo of his child's actual birthday. He was only off by three days.

The non-laboring wife of a lesbian couple that I cared for through 4+ hours of pushing, had full sleeves of gorgeous, brightly colored flowers. It gave us a lot to talk about.

A mom of three had a beautiful set of lips tattooed on her lower abdomen as a teenager. When pregnant, those lips stretched from about 2'x 5" to 4'x 10". Her stretch marks provided perfect lip lines, which we still talk about today, almost 20 years later.

And an all-time favorite—the patient was completely shaved except for about 1 cm at the top of her pubic hairline with a stick figure on one side pushing a lawnmower. After I laughed, I told her I was going to tell my sister-in-law to get this same tattoo because her family owns a lawn care company.

Epilogue

Although the birth stories flowed from my memory with vivid detail, I regret not having kept a record of each birth I had the privilege of witnessing throughout my career. How many? Likely thousands. This includes deliveries where I spent hours (and on rare occasions- consecutive days) with the patient, and those where I was present for just a few minutes, sometimes as a "secondary" baby nurse. I wonder how many were boys? How many were girls? How many were born alive? How many were stillborn? I celebrate the routine dimensions of birthing experienced by the majority of patients and I honor the losses and challenges faced by those who have endured such difficult circumstances. Overall, I felt incredibly fortunate to be in a space where the pulse of life—whether strong, faint, distorted, or dying—was present in infants, mothers, support persons and hospital staff. I shared moments of laughter, tears of joy and sorrow, not only with my patients but also with my fellow staff members. What a truly dynamic and rewarding career.

As I wrote this book and reflected upon the meaning of my career, I recognized the crucial role of embedding a sense of purpose, a *why*, into my actions as a nurse. While learning what to do was relatively easy, I came to realize that knowing *why* was far more essential. Since writing this book, I have rediscovered my sense of purpose in mentoring and inspiring both current and future nurses and medical professionals, much like I did when I helped orient new nurses or "raised" new OB residents.

Throughout my career, I've witnessed considerable changes, both in my personal life and within the hospital environment. As a young nurse, my response to various situations was shaped by my limited experience and the policies and procedures of that era. The healthcare setting was quite different then: for instance, it's hard to imagine that when I first started working at the hospital, managing climate control meant contending with clouds of cigarette smoke in both patient rooms and the cafeteria. The approach to care was more conventional with less focus on holistic patient care.

Over the years, both the fields of nursing and medicine and my own approach evolved considerably. Experience and maturity played pivotal roles in this evolution. As I gained a deeper understanding and developed a stronger trust in my intuition, I became better equipped to navigate complex situations with greater insight and empathy. As a passionate patient advocate, I learned to choose my battles carefully and fight for what mattered, no matter the challenges involved. Additionally, my own therapy played a crucial role in my healing and personal growth, helping me to better process challenges, enhance my emotional resilience and improve how I approached both professional and personal situations.

I want to convey how profoundly meaningful it was to forge such deep connections with both my patients and my work family. As we shared these sacred birth moments together, our relationships strengthened as we united in our efforts to achieve the best possible outcomes in these profound human experiences. It wasn't until my retirement that I fully appreciated how unique, powerful and unmatched the energy we shared truly was.

Witnessing childbirth involves interacting with parents, grandparents, family, friends and newborns, creating relationships and connections that foster growth. This experience can be overwhelming because not all families are prepared for such intense emotions and dynamics. To support families through this process and to make their experience spiritually enriching, I learned that I needed to embrace the complexity of emotions, including love and grief, happiness and sorrow. Providing both emotional and physical support was essential. Additionally, fostering an environment where strength and vulnerability could coexist was important, allowing families to express and process their feelings openly.

I named my first daughter Elizabeth. Because I had chosen closed adoption, I didn't know who had adopted her or where she had been raised. When she was 18 years old, I contacted the adoption agency and discovered that she had grown up 5 miles from where I lived and that she wanted to meet me. After a few phone calls with her, her parents invited me and my family to their home to meet in person.

Although I was understandably anxious about this encounter of meeting Elizabeth for the first time, I was not prepared to encounter my buried grief. I felt that I didn't deserve to grieve, because I had *chosen* adoption. I knew this to be very different from the experience of parents who face the sudden loss of a child due to an unexpected death or a tragic birth outcome. Their profound grief, something these parents would never choose, is widely recognized, as it should be. I struggled with guilt, questioning the legitimacy of my neatly packaged, self-inflicted grief.

In fact, I distinctly remember the first time I felt this intense grief. I was sitting at the kitchen table after our first phone call in 2001. The reconnection brought with it a swirl of ambiguous emotions: the joy of hearing my daughter's voice again, a sound I hadn't heard since I swaddled and handed her to the adoption caseworker. At the same time, there was the piercing fear of losing her once more just as I had finally found and reconnected with her.

The emotions stirred by this momentous event, along with other indicators in my life, convinced me to start therapy. I went to counseling with a list of things to work on and goals to achieve. *This won't surprise anyone who knows me.* What I eventually discovered, with the guidance of a wise and experienced therapist, was the deep and multifaceted nature of my grief. Simply put, grief is love with nowhere to go. I realized how much I had blocked deeper intimate connections with others including my own children and husband by protecting myself and burying my losses. In other words, I learned that to the extent that grief is blocked, love is hindered. The more we love the more we grieve. As I confronted the layers of pain and grief stemming from my parents' divorce, my father's abandonment, and my mother's struggle with addiction, I was better able to offer myself compassion. This compassion extended to the difficult situation and impossible choice my nurse, Karen, helped me grapple with decades ago–alone in a rural hospital. I am truly grateful for the opportunity to build a relationship with Elizabeth and her family, which has blossomed and evolved over the past 23 years, despite the fact that we live in different parts of the country.

The writing of this book not only shares the remarkable stories of birth and my nursing career, it has helped me to clarify my calling to become a labor and delivery nurse in the first place; it has deepened my understanding of my journey to heal myself and embrace the chance for a greater life. Additionally, it deepened my commitment to honor the challenge my late Grandma Eleanor gave me: to stay humbly present and curious in each unfolding moment, because life is bountifully short and *I'll Never See it All.*

This book is my way of giving back to everyone who has been part of the journey through birth, grief, hope and love.

END

References

ABC Law Centers. (n.d.). What Are Normal Umbilical Cord Blood Gas Results? ABC Law Centers. Retrieved from https://www.abclawcenters.com/frequently-asked-questions/what-are-normal-umbilical-cord-blood-gas-results/#:~:text=values%20are%20normal.-,pH, other%20forms%20of%20 brain%20damage.

Clark, S., Nageotte, M., Garite, T., Freeman, R., Miller, D. A., Simpson, K. R., Belfort, M., Dildy, G., Parer, J., Berkowitz, R. L., D'Alton, M., Rouse, D. J., Gilstrap, L., Vintzileos, A., van Dorsten, J., Boehm, F. H., Miller, L. A. and Hankins, G. (2013). 'Intrapartum Management of Category II Fetal Heart Rate Tracings: Toward Standardization of Care'. Semantic Scholar. Retrieved from https://www.semanticscholar.org/paper/Intrapartum-management-of-category-II-fetal-heart-Clark-Nageotte/ce276a4cd83d710f8ca62fb5a02dfa6804716fed

Cleveland Clinic. (n.d.). Meconium. Cleveland Clinic. Retrieved from
https://my.clevelandclinic.org/health/body/24102-meconium.

MedlinePlus. (n.d.). Apgar score. MedlinePlus. https://medlineplus.gov/ency/article/003402.htm

Missouri Baptist Medical Center. (n.d.). Safe Warm. Missouri Baptist Medical Center. Retrieved from *https://www.missouribaptist.org/Medical-Services/Childbirth-Center/Childbirth-Center-Post/ArtMID/541/ArticleID/235/Safe-Warm*

National Certification Corporation. (2010, April 29). NICHD Definitions and Classifications: Application to Electronic Fetal Monitoring Interpretation. Retrieved from https://www.nccwebsite.org/content/documents/cms/final_ncc_monograph_web-4-29-10.pdf.